D0119054

AMERICAN Family Treasury

Every house where love abides
And friendship is a guest
Is truly home, and home sweet home,
For there the heart can rest.

Henry van Dyke

Ideals Publications Incorporated
Nashville, Tennessee

Publisher, Patricia A. Pingry; Editor, Nancy J. Skarmeas;
Art Director, Patrick T. McRae; Copy Editor, Donna Sigalos Budjenska

Art by Stacey Venturi-Pickett

Acknowledgments

THE SCHOOL OF PRAYER from MAMA'S WAY by Thyra Ferre Bjorn. Copyright ©1959 by Thyra Ferre Bjorn. Reprinted by permission of Henry Holt and Company, Inc.; OUR FEATHERED FRIENDS from MY SISTER EILEEN, copyright ©1938 and renewed 1966 by Ruth McKenney, reprinted by permission of Harcourt Brace Jovanovich, Inc.; HOW BEAUTIFUL WITH MUD from WE SHOOK THE FAMILY TREE by Hildegarde Dolson. Copyright ©1941, 1942, 1946 and renewed 1970 by Hildegarde Dolson. Reprinted by permission of Random House, Inc.; FATHER'S HARD-ROCKING SHIP from THE BEST OF CLARENCE DAY by Clarence Day. Copyright ©1948 by Mrs. Katherine B. Day. Reprinted by permission of Alfred A. Knopf, Inc.; MY WILD IRISH MOTHER from HOW I GOT TO BE PERFECT by Jean Kerr. Copyright ©1978 by Collins Productions, Inc. Used by permission of Doubleday, a division of Bantam Doubleday Dell Publishing Group, Inc.; ALL OVER from FATHER OF THE BRIDE by Edward Streeter. Copyright ©1949 by Edward Streeter and Gluyas Williams and renewed 1976 by Edward Streeter. Reprinted by permission of Simon & Schuster; OUR SILLY LITTLE SISTER by Dorothy Aldis reprinted by permission of G.P. Putnam's Sons from ALL TOGETHER, copyright ©1925-1928, 1934, 1939, 1952, copyright renewed 1953-6, ©1962 by Dorothy Aldis, ©1967, ©1980 by Roy E. Porter.; WHAT A BABY COSTS by Edgar A. Guest from A HEAP O' LIVIN', copyright ©1916 by The Reilly & Britton Co. Used by permission of the author's estate; SUMMERTIME from LITTLE HOUSE IN THE BIG WOODS by Laura Ingalls Wilder. Copyright ©1932 by Laura Ingalls Wilder. Copyright © renewed 1960 by Roger L. MacBride. Reprinted by permission of HarperCollins Publishers; INDEPENDENCE DAY from FARMER BOY by Laura Ingalls Wilder. Copyright ©1933 by Laura Ingalls Wilder. Copyright © renewed 1961 by Roger L. MacBride. Reprinted by permission of HarperCollins Publishers; HIS GOOD STEPMOTHER by Genevieve Foster. Reprinted with the permission of Charles Scribner's Sons, an imprint of Macmillan Publishing Company from ABRAHAM LINCOLN by Genevieve Foster. Copyright ©1950 Genevieve Foster; copyright renewed ©1978 Genevieve Foster; THE LINCOLN PETS from WHITE HOUSE PETS by Margaret Truman. Copyright ©1969 by David McKay Company, Inc. Reprinted by permission of the author and the author's agents, Scott Meredith Literary Agency, Inc., 845 Third Avenue, New York, New York 10022; TR: CHILDREN'S HERO from THEODORE ROOSEVELT: THE MAN AS I KNEW HIM by Nicholas Roosevelt. Copyright ©1967 by Dodd, Mead & Company. Used by permission of the author's estate; ON BEING A GRANDDAUGHTER from BLACKBERRY WINTER by Margaret Mead. Copyright ©1972 by Margaret Mead. Reprinted by permission of William Morrow & Co., Inc.; FAMILY LIFE IN THE WHITE HOUSE from UPSTAIRS AT THE WHITE HOUSE: MY LIFE WITH THE FIRST LADIES by J.B. West. Copyright ©1973 by J.B. West. Reprinted by permission of Ms. Zella West.

Artists and Photographers

George Hinke: cover, pages 17, 21, 27, 39, 54, 66, 86–87, 93, 107. Frances Hook: pages 29, 30, 41, 43, 44, 83, 96. Richard Hook: pages 9, 14, 19, 32, 46, 70, 78, 99, 103. John McClelland: page 37. Scwalb Photography: pages 115, 117, 119, 121, 123, 125, 127, 129. John Walter: pages 11, 35, 53, 58, 62, 81, 109. Ann Williams: chapter openings.

Text copy set in Sabon; Display type set in Bookman Swash
Color separations by Rayson Films, Waukesha, Wisconsin

ISBN 0-8249-4049-0

CONTENTS

FAMILIES FROM ANY NEIGHBORHOOD

Home Sweet Home

Learning how to drive.
Aunt Suzanne
& Buddy.

Helen at 6 months.

The new car.

Grandma, Santa,
+ June

The Big Day

The School of Prayer

from *Mama's Way* by Thyra Ferre Bjorn

My training to serve God began in the school of prayer, which is the strongest power on earth. As my mind wanders back into my childhood days, and memories unfold as pages in a book, I remember how Mama brought us eight children up on prayer. She served it both as a full-course meal and as snacks in between.

Mama was impatient in her praying. She was never willing to wait for things, but expected an immediate answer. Papa seemed to leave the outcome up to God. If he could not see an answer, he accepted that as God's wisdom, and no doubt clouded his faith in God's power. Perhaps, I reasoned with myself, it was the things they prayed about that made a difference. To Mama, prayer came as easy as breathing. Even if she knew people termed her prayer method strange and naive, it never seemed to bother her. She kept on praying that the cake she had placed in the oven would not fall and that the food would stretch a long way because there were so many to feed at one table. And there was the long line of people who depended upon her help and came to ask her to take their problems to God for them. These people surely believed that God would answer them through Mama. They felt that in some strange way she was "in" with God and that He would grant her what He would refuse them. So prayers would be sent out for a quick sale of their house, for a husband to be kinder to his wife, and children to recover from their colds. I often heard her prayers and saw the people coming, and I never remember one who went away disappointed. Things did change when Mama talked with God.

Of course, Papa, as a minister, had certain prayer projects. His prayers were always as sincere as he was himself, and many people came to his study with their prayer problems. Then there were the sickbed prayers where he made his daily calls. Papa's prayers seemed to me loftier than Mama's. They were bigger prayers! Still, when Papa prayed for the man who had a bad case of lumbago, and was in pain day and night, he seemed to get worse instead of better. He wasn't healed. And how can I ever forget that lovely wife with a devoted husband and their family of five small children? Knowing she was at death's door, Papa prayed for her all night long. All hope was gone, but my Papa prayed on, torn by fatigue and compassion. But the wife died. Could God answer only small prayers? I wondered. I felt sorry for Papa. . . .

Then came another discouraging experience. This time it was one of my sisters, who had a panicky fear of the dentist. Having observed Mama's way of talking to God, she hit upon a bright idea. There was no need to tell Mama and Papa that she had a big cavity in her tooth. She would go directly to God and tell Him about it and ask Him to do the work on it. It would be wonderful! There would be no more suffering in the dentist's chair. Mama had always said that nothing was impossible for God to do. My sister decided to try it that very night; she would set forth alone on this prayer adventure.

"Please, please, God," she prayed as she knelt by her bed, "fill my tooth. Fill it good and hard . . . and do the work while I sleep. I want it all filled when I wake up in the morning. Thank you for being so good to me . . . and I shall always try to be a good girl. Amen."

The next morning when she awoke, she

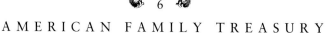

slid her tongue over the spot where the cavity had been. It wasn't there—the tooth was filled. She was healed! Breathless with excitement, she rushed out to Mama in the kitchen.

"Mama, Mama," she cried, "God has done it again!"

Mama stopped beating the eggs and gazed with surprise at her young daughter. "He has done what?" she asked.

"He filled my tooth last night, Mama, when I asked Him to. . .."

Mama patted the excited girl on her blonde head. She asked to be shown the miracle and, equipped with a toothpick, she poked at the tooth. It didn't take her long to come to a verdict. She looked tenderly down at her offspring as she held the toothpick in front of her eyes. "It wasn't God this time, darling." She smiled. "Your tooth was filled with a piece of bread."

I surely felt as though God and Mama had both let my little sister down, but Papa explained something to us that morning around the breakfast table. And he gave us a clear understanding of how God works through prayer. God was a wise God, he said, and everything in His world was made in order. Dentists had been given their skill by God to help people, and children should be thankful they could go to them when they had a bad toothache. It wasn't that God couldn't . . . it was that He didn't choose to. My sister's prayer had been a foolish, selfish prayer and not one to honor God.

Little by little I seemed to grasp more of this strange power that we earth people use to contact God for the good of the world we live in. But I still didn't really know what prayer was until one day I accompanied Papa on a call to an old man's shack on a cold fall afternoon. . . .

The man was bedridden, crippled up with aches and pains. His shack was very primitive. He insisted that Papa make coffee for us. So Papa put on the muddy-looking coffeepot and found some cookies, and although they were musty looking and smelled funny, he ate two. I didn't want any, but one look made me understand it would be very rude not to eat one. It might hurt the man's feelings. After we had had our coffee and had served the old man some, too, we sat down by his bed and Papa read from the Bible about the lame man that the Master healed. After the reading, we knelt to pray.

Papa prayed first. It was a long prayer. I soon lost track of it and escaped into my own imaginative world. Then suddenly, Papa nudged me to indicate that I was to pray, too. I meant it from my heart when I asked God to make the man well, and I even thanked God for the musty cookie . . .

Then the man prayed. He clasped his disfigured hands and lifted his face heavenward. Something very special came into his voice, and although it was against the rule, I opened my eyes to peek just a wee bit at him. I couldn't figure it out, but his face changed as he prayed. It was radiant with joy, almost shiny, and my eyes opened wider and wider. That man never asked to be healed. He didn't ask God for anything. He just thanked Him as though he had been given everything in the whole world. He thanked God for the poor

I surely felt as though God and Mama had both let my little sister down, but Papa explained something to us that morning around the breakfast table. And he gave us a clear understanding of how God works through prayer.

7

little shack in which he lived, for his warm bed, and for the kind people who dropped in to care for him. He prayed for his pastor and the blessing he had brought in coming out to read and pray with him, and even for this little girl who prayed so sweetly. He went on thanking God for the birds in the branches of the big tree outside his window and the snow that soon would come and make the world white; for summer and its beauty and this windy fall day that made him feel snug and sheltered in his room where he was sure of God's protection day and night. I never closed my eyes again during his prayer because I loved to see how quickly he kept changing as he talked to God. When we bade him good-bye, he looked as happy and contented as though he had no discomfort at all. And where before his face had been twisted with pain, it now looked relaxed and joyous.

"My girl," he said, "prayers are the thoughts that come forth from our inner being. Prayer is our highest self, the very best within us. . . For once we are absolutely honest, . . . we can hide nothing from God."

How could it have happened? I wondered, perplexed. How could words tossed into the air make such a difference? The man was still sick, but that prayer had taken the sadness out of him. I realized that the change must have been within his heart—it was the joy from a happy inside that shone through. On the way home I asked Papa to explain prayer to me. And Papa did his best to try to come down to my level.

"My girl," he said, "prayers are the thoughts that come forth from our inner being. Prayer is our highest self, the very best within us that comes out in words from our lips. For once we are absolutely honest, knowing that we can hide nothing from God. As we pray, we become humble and sincere and there is a desire deep within us to be good. Forming prayer into words makes it more tangible. The words form a contact with God, so that our eyes reflect a glimpse of His glory. The heart beats with joy, for we know in God there is help for all our problems."

I walked silently beside my papa for a long time. He had talked to me as if I were a grownup, and I was proud and happy. The wind blew in the treetops. It was bitter cold. My feet ached now and I felt as if there were little stones in my shoes. It was getting dark. Papa still held my hand in his. His words are true, I was thinking; prayer must be like that. I had seen it in the old man's face. When he had made the contact with his God, he had forgotten his pain and loneliness. His aches were still there, but he could bear them with courage. Perhaps, I thought, that was a greater answer than to be made well.

"Look, dear," said Papa. "See the lights over there in the village. See, there is the parsonage—Mama just lit the lamp. Soon we will be home!"

It's like prayer, I was thinking, as my heart beat fast in the gladness of this new thought. Prayer is like walking in the dark and suddenly seeing a lamp being lit to tell you home is there. In prayer, God is waiting for us, just as in the parsonage Mama was waiting for Papa and me. She knew we would be cold and hungry and tired, and she would meet us with open arms to welcome us home. It would be warm inside those walls, and clean and homey. Good food would be cooking on the stove. Mama would take my shoes off and warm my feet, placing soft slippers on them. I could see it all in my mind as I walked with Papa toward the light. ❧

FAMILIES FROM ANY NEIGHBORHOOD

Our Feathered Friends

from *My Sister Eileen* by Ruth McKenney

From childhood, my sister and I have had a well-grounded dislike for our friends the birds. We came to hate them when she was ten and I was eleven. We had been exiled by what we considered an unfeeling family to one of those loathsome girls' camps where Indian lore is rife and the management puts up neatly lettered signs reminding the clients to be Good Sports. From the moment Eileen and I arrived at dismal old Camp Hi-Wah, we were Bad Sports, and we liked it. . . .

Bird Life for Children was a volume that all Good Citizens in Camp Hi-Wah pretended to find engrossing. Eileen and I thought it was stupefyingly dull. . . . *Bird Life for Children* was full of horrid pictures in full-color of robins and pigeons and redbirds. We hated the book, so we were quite prepared to despise birds when we started off that morning on our first bird walk, but we had no idea that we were going to suffer, that whole awful summer, because of our feathered friends. . . .

On that first bird walk, Eileen and I trotted anxiously behind the little band of serious-minded bird-lovers, trying desperately to see, or at least hear, even one bird, even one robin. But alas, while other bird-walkers saw, or pretended to see—for Eileen and I never believed them for a moment—all kinds of hummingbirds and hawks and owls and whatnot, we never saw or heard a single, solitary feathered friend, not one. . . .

For the next three days we stayed honest and suffered. For three terrible mornings we endured being dolts among bird-walkers, the laughing-stock of Camp Hi-Wah. After six incredibly tiresome hours, our bird logs were still blank. Then we cracked under the strain. The fourth morning we got up feeling grim but determined. We sharpened our pencils before we started off on the now-familiar trail through the second-growth forest.

When we got well into the woods and Mary Mahoney, the premier bird-walker of Camp Hi-Wah, had already spotted and logged her first redbird of the morning, Eileen suddenly stopped dead in her tracks. "Hark!" she cried. She had read that somewhere in a book. "Quiet!" I echoed instantly.

The bird-walkers drew to a halt respectfully and stood in silence. They stood and stood. It was not good form even to whisper while other bird-walkers were logging a victim, but after quite a long time, the Leader, whose feet were flat and often hurt her, whispered impatiently, "Haven't you got him logged yet?"

"You drove him away," Eileen replied sternly. "It was a yellow-bellied cuckoo."

"A yellow-bellied cuckoo?" cried the Leader incredulously.

"Well," Eileen said modestly, "at least I think it was." Then with pretty hesitation and thoughtful pause, she recited the leading features of the yellow-bellied cuckoo as recorded in *Bird Life for Children*.

The Leader was terribly impressed. Later on that morning I logged a kingfisher, a redheaded woodpecker, and a yellow-bellied sapsucker, which was all I could remember at the moment. Each time, I kept the bird-walkers standing around for an interminable period, gaping into blank space and listening desperately to the rustle of the wind in the trees and the creak of their shoes as they went from one foot to another. . . .

We had begun to get pretty bored with logging new birds when the game took on a

10

new angle. Mary Mahoney and several other bird-walkers began to see the same birds we did on our morning jaunts into the forest. This made us pretty mad, but there wasn't much we could do about it. Next, Mary Mahoney began to see birds we weren't logging. The third week after we joined the Camp Hi-Wah Bird Study Circle, everybody except the poor, dumb leader and a few backward but honest bird-lovers was logging the rarest birds seen around Camp Hi-Wah in twenty years. . . .

The poor bird-walk Leader was in agony. Her reputation as a bird-lover was in shreds. Her talented pupils were seeing rare birds right and left, while the best she could log for herself would be a few crummy old redbirds and a robin or so. At last our Leader's morale collapsed. . . . "I can't see any nightingale," our Leader cried, and burst into tears. Then, full of shame, she sped back to camp, leaving the Camp Hi-Wah bird-lovers to their nightingales and guilty thoughts.

Eileen and I ate a hearty lunch that noon because we thought we would need it. Then we strolled down Hiawatha Alley and hunted up Mary Mahoney.

"We will put the Iron Cross on you if you tell," Eileen started off as soon as we found Mary.

"What's the Iron Cross?" Mary squeaked, startled out of her usual haughty poise.

"Never mind," I growled. "You'll find out if you tell."

We walked past Cabin Sitting Bull, past the flagpole, into the tall grass beyond the ballfield.

"She'll tell," Eileen said finally.

"What'll we do?" I replied mournfully. "They'll try us at campfire tonight."

They did, too. It was terrible. We denied everything, but the Head of Camp, a mean old lady who wore middy blouses and pleated serge bloomers, sentenced us to no desserts and eight o'clock bedtime for two weeks. We thought over what to do to Mary Mahoney for four whole days. Nothing seemed sufficiently frightful, but in the end we put the wart curse on her. The wart curse was simple but horrible. We dropped around to Cabin Sitting Bull one evening and in the presence of Mary and her allies we drew ourselves up to our full height and said solemnly and in unison, "We put the wart curse on you, Mary Mahoney." Then we stalked away.

We didn't believe for a moment in the wart curse, but we hoped Mary would. At first she was openly contemptuous, but to our delight, on the fourth evening, she developed a horrible sty in her eye. We told everybody a sty was a kind of wart and that we had Mary in our power. The next day Mary broke down and came around to our cabin and apologized in choked accents. She gave Eileen her best hair ribbon and me a little barrel that had a picture of Niagara Falls inside it, if you looked hard enough. We were satisfied. ✺

How Beautiful with Mud

from *We Shook the Family Tree* by Hildegarde Dolson

Perhaps the surest way to tell when a female goes over the boundary from childhood into meaningful adolescence is to watch how long it takes her to get to bed at night. My own cross-over, which could be summed up in our family as "What on earth is Hildegarde *doing* in the bathroom?," must have occurred when I was a freshman in high school. Until then, I fell into bed dog-tired each night, after the briefest possible bout with toothbrush and washcloth. But once I'd become aware of the Body Beautiful, as portrayed in advertisements in women's magazines, my absorption was complete and my attitude highly optimistic. I too would be beautiful. I would also be Flower-Fresh, Fastidious, and Dainty—a triple-threat virtue obviously prized above pearls by the entire male sex, as depicted in the *Ladies' Home Journal*.

Somehow, out of my dollar-a-week allowance, I managed to buy Mum, Odorono, Listerine, and something called Nipso, the latter guaranteed to remove excess hair from arms and legs, and make a man think, "Oooo, what a flawless surface." It's true that I had no men, nor was I a particularly hairy child, having only light yellow down on my angular appendages. Nevertheless, I applied the Nipso painstakingly in the bathroom one night with Sally as my interested audience. I had noticed the stuff had a rather overpowering, sickish-sweet scent, but this was a very minor drawback, considering the goal I had in mind. After Sally had been watching me for a few minutes, she began holding her nose. Finally she asked me to unlock the door and let her out. "Don't you want to see me wash it off?" I asked, rather hurt.

"No," Sally said. "It smells funny."

In the next hour, as my father, mother, and brothers followed their noses to the upstairs hall, there were far more detailed descriptions of how Nipso affected the olfactory senses. . . .

I already had my eye on something that sounded far more fascinating than Nipso. This was a miraculous substance called Beauty Clay, and every time I read about it in a magazine advertisement, the words enveloped me in rapture. Even the story of its discovery was a masterpiece in lyrical prose. Seems this girl was traveling in an obscure European country (name on request) and ran out of things that ladies always run out of at the wrong time, such as powder and make-up lotion. The worst part was that the girl really needed such artifices to cover up bumps. Through some intuitive process which escapes me at the moment, she had the presence of mind to go to a nearby hamlet, pick up a handful of mud, and plaster it on her face. Then she lay dozing in the sun, by a brook. When she came to, washed the clay-like mud off her face, and looked at her reflection in the brook, she knew she had hit the jackpot. Boy, was she beautiful. Looking at the Before-and-After pictures, I could see that this beauty was more than skin-deep, having benefited even her nose, eyes, and hair.

After pondering all this, I could well understand why a jar of the imported Beauty Clay cost $4.98. In fact, it was dirt cheap at the price, and my only problem was how to lay my hands on $4.98. . . . Due to the fact that I had such important things as Beauty Clay on my mind, it was understandable that my monthly marks in algebra should cause even more distress than usual in the bosom

of my family. . . . I honestly meant well, and I even went so far as to carry books home from school and carry them back again the next morning. But freshman algebra, implying as it did that X equals Y, was simply beyond me. Finally my father said that if I got on the Honor Roll he'd give me five dollars. Wobbly as I was in mathematics, it took me only a flash to realize this sum was approximately equal to $4.98, or the piddling price of Beauty Clay. From here on in, I was straining every muscle. When I say that I got 89 in algebra and climbed to the bottom rung of the Honor Roll, I am stating a miracle simply. What is more important, I got the five bucks.

My father said that if I liked, he'd put most of it in my savings account. Bobby said, with even more enthusiasm, that he knew where I could get a bargain in a second-hand pistol. I declined both offers, marveling at the things men could think of to do with money, and made my way, on foot, to Riesenman's Drugstore. When Mr. Riesenman said he had no Beauty Clay, I was grieved. When he said he'd never even heard of the stuff, I was appalled. It took three trips to convince him that he must order it immediately, money on the line. . . .

It took a week before I could achieve the needed privacy for my quick-change act. Mother was taking Jimmy and Sally downtown to get new shoes. Bobby was going skiing, and my father, as usual, would be at the office. I got home to the empty house at twenty minutes of four, and made a bee-line for the Beauty Clay. . . .

The Beauty Clay was a rather peculiar shade of grayish-green, and I spread this all over my face and neck—"even to the hairline where tell-tale wrinkles hide." The directions also urged me not to talk or smile during the twenty minutes it would take for the clay to dry. The last thing in the world I wanted to do was talk or smile. That could come later. For now, a reverent silence would suffice. . . .

According to the clock, the Beauty Clay had been on the required twenty minutes, and was now ready to be washed off. It occurred to me that if twenty minutes was enough to make me beautiful, thirty minutes or even forty minutes would make me twice as beautiful. Besides, it would give me more lovely moments of anticipation, and Mother wouldn't be home till after five.

By the time my face was so rigid that even my eyeballs felt yanked from their sockets, I knew I must be done, on both sides. As I started back to the bathroom, I heard Bobby's voice downstairs yelling "Mom!" With the haste born of horror I ran back and just managed to bolt myself inside the bathroom as Bobby leaped up the stairs and down the hall towards his room. Then I turned on the faucets and set to work. The directions had particularly warned "Use only gentle splashes to remove the mask—No rubbing or washcloth." It took several minutes of gentle splashing to make me realize this was getting me nowhere fast. Indeed, it was like splashing playfully at the Rock of Gibralter. I decided that maybe it wouldn't hurt if I rubbed the beauty mask just a little, with a nailbrush. This hurt only the nailbrush. I myself remained embedded in Beauty Clay.

By this time, I was getting worried. Mother would be home very soon and I needed a face—even any old face. Suddenly it occurred to me that a silver knife would be a big help, although I wasn't sure just how. When I heard Bobby moving around in his room, I yelled at him to bring me a knife from the dining room sideboard. Rather, that's what I intended to yell, but my facial muscles were still cast in stone, and the most I could do was grunt. In desperation, I ran down to the sideboard, tripping over my sheet as I went, and got the knife. Unfortunately, just as I was coming back through the dusky upstairs hall, Bobby walked out of his room and met me, face to face. The men-

13

tal impact, on Bobby, was terrific. To do him justice, he realized almost instantly that this was his own sister, and not, as he at first imagined, a sea monster. But even this realization was not too reassuring.

I had often imagined how my family would look at me after the Beauty Clay had taken effect. Now it had taken effect—or even permanent possession of me—and Bobby was certainly reacting, but not quite as I'd pictured it.

"Wh—what?" he finally managed to croak, pointing at my face.

His concern was so obvious and even comforting that I tried to explain what had happened. The sounds that came out alarmed him even more.

Not having the time or the necessary freedom of speech to explain any further, I dashed into the bathroom and began hitting the handle of the knife against my rocky visage. To my heavenly relief, it began to crack. After repeated blows, which made me a little groggy, the stuff had broken up enough to allow me to wriggle my jaw. Meanwhile, Bobby stood at the door watching, completely bemused.

Taking advantage of the cracks in my surface, I dug the blade of the knife in, and by scraping, gouging, digging, and prying, I got part of my face clear. As soon as I could talk, I turned on Bobby. "If you tell anybody about this, I'll kill you," I said fiercely.

Whether it was the intensity of my threat or latent chivalry aroused by seeing a lady tortured before his very eyes, I still don't know, but Bobby said, "Cross my heart and hope to die." . . .

When Mother saw my scarlet, splotched face, she exclaimed in concern. "Why Hildegarde, are you feverish?" She made a move to feel my forehead, but I backed away. I was burning up, but not with fever.

"I'm alright," I said, applying myself to setting the table. With my face half in the china cupboard, I mumbled that I'd been frostbitten and had rubbed myself with snow.

"Oh, Cliff," Mother called. "Little Hildegarde was frostbitten." . . .

Bobby had followed me out to the kitchen to see how the frostbite story went over. As Mother kept exclaiming over my condition he now said staunchly, "Sure she's all right. Let her alone."

My father and mother both stared at him, in this new role of Big Brother Galahad. In fact, my father reacted rather cynically. "Bobby, did you and your friends knock Hildegarde down and rub her face with snow?"

"Me? " Bobby squeaked. He gave me a dirty look, as if to say, "You'd better talk fast."

I denied hotly that Bobby had done any such thing. In fact, I proceeded to build him up as my sole rescuer, a great big St. Bernard of a brother who had come bounding through the snow drifts to bring me life and hope.

Bobby looked so gratified at what he'd been through in my story that I knew my secret was safe.

Sally, always an affectionate child, began to sob. "She might have died. Bobby saved her from freezing."

My father and mother remained dry-eyed. Against this new set-up of Brother Loves Sister they were suspicious, but inclined to do nothing.

And in a way, I had been frostbitten, to the quick. Lying in bed that night, still smarting, I tried to think up ways to get even. It wasn't clear to me exactly whom or what I had to get even with. All I knew was that I was sore and unbeautiful, and mulcted of five dollars. With the hot and cold fury of a woman stung, I suddenly conceived my plan for revenge. It was so simple and logical and yet brilliant that my mind relaxed at last. Some day I, too, would write advertisements.

Father's Hard-Rocking Ship

from *Life with Father* by Clarence Day

Father said that one great mystery about the monthly household expenses was what made them jump up and down so. "Anyone would suppose that there would be some regularity after a while which would let a man try to make plans, but I never know from one month to another what to expect."

Mother said she didn't, either. Things just seemed to go that way.

"But they have no business to go that way, Vinnie," Father declared. "And what's more I won't allow it."

Mother said she didn't see what she could do about it. All she knew is that when the bills mounted up, it didn't mean that she had been extravagant. . . .

Appearances were often hopelessly against Mother, but that never daunted her. She wasn't afraid of Father or anybody. She was a woman of great spirit who would have flown at and pecked any tyrant. It was only when she had a bad conscience that she had no heart to fight. Father had the best of her there because he never had a bad conscience.

When the household expenses shot up very high, Father got frightened. He would then, as Mother put it, yell his head off. He always did some yelling anyhow, merely on general principles, but when his alarm was genuine he roared in real anguish.

Usually this brought the total down again, at least for awhile. But there were times when no amount of noise seemed to do any good, and when every month, for one reason or another, the total went up and up. And then, just when Father had resigned himself to this awful outgo, and just as he had eased up on his yelling and had begun to feel grim, the expenses, to his utter amaze-ment, would take a sharp drop. . . .

When he told her, he did it in as disciplinary a manner as possible. He didn't congratulate her on the expenses having come down. He appeared at her door, waving the bills at her with a threatening scowl, and said, "I've told you again and again that you could keep expenses down if you tried, and this shows I was right." . . .

He had at last invented what seemed a perfect method of recording expenses. Whenever he gave any money to Mother, he asked her what it was for and made a note of it in his pocket notebook. His idea was that these items, added to those in the itemized bills, would show him exactly where every dollar had gone.

But they didn't.

He consulted his notebook. "I gave you six dollars in cash on the twenty-fifth of last month," he said, "to buy a new coffeepot."

"Yes," Mother said, "because you broke the old one. You threw it right on the floor."

Father frowned. "I'm not talking about that," he answered. "I am simply endeavoring to find out from you, if I can—" "But it's so silly to break a nice coffeepot, Clare, and that was the last of those French ones, and there was nothing the matter with the coffee that morning; it was made just the same as it always is."

"It wasn't," said Father. "It was made in a . . . barbaric manner."

"And I couldn't get another French one," Mother continued, "because that little shop the Auffmordts told us about has stopped selling them. They said the tariff wouldn't let them any more, and I told Monsieur Duval he ought to be ashamed of himself to stand there and say so. I said that if I had a shop, I'd like to see the tariff keep me from selling

AMERICAN FAMILY TREASURY

things."

"But I gave you six dollars to buy a new pot," Father firmly repeated, "and now I find that you apparently got one at Lewis and Conger's and charged it. Here's the bill: 'one brown earthenware drip coffeepot, five dollars.'"

"So I saved you a dollar," Mother said triumphantly, "and you can hand it right over.'" . . .

She came home one afternoon in a terrible state. "Has it come yet?" she asked the waitress.

The waitress said nothing had come that she knew of.

Mother ran upstairs with a hunted expression and flung herself down on the bed. When we looked in, she was sobbing.

It turned out she had gone to an auction, and she had become so excited that she had bought but not paid for a grandfather's clock.

Mother knew in her heart that she had no business going

to auctions. . . . an auction aroused all her worst instincts—her combativeness, her recklessness, and her avaricious love of a bargain. And the worst part about it was that this time it wasn't a bargain at all. The awful old thing was eight feet tall, and it wasn't the one she had wanted. . . . inside the hood over the dial, she said, there was a little ship which at first she hadn't noticed, a horrid ship that rocked up and down every time the clock ticked. It made her ill just to look at it. And she didn't have the money, and the man said he'd have to send it this evening, and what would Father say?

She could hardly believe it, but she found that luck was with her, for once. If the clock

had come earlier there may have been a major catastrophe, but Father was in a good mood and he had had a good dinner. And though he never admitted it or spoke of it, he had a weakness for clocks . . . . So when Mother led him out into the hall to confess to him and show him what she had bought, and he saw that it was a clock, he fell in love with it, and made almost no fuss at all.

The letdown was too much for Mother. She tottered off to her room without another word and went straight to bed, leaving Father and the auctioneer's man setting up the new clock alongside the hat rack. Father was especially fascinated by the hard-rocking ship.

FAMILIES FROM ANY NEIGHBORHOOD

My Wild Irish Mother

from *How I Got to Be Perfect* by Jean Kerr

I'm never going to write my autobiography, and it's all my mother's fault. I didn't hate her, so I have practically no material. In fact, the situation is worse than I'm pretending. We were crazy about her—and you know I'll never get a book out of that, much less a musical.

Mother was born Kitty O'Neill in Kinsale, Ireland, with bright red hair, bright blue eyes, and the firm conviction that it was wrong to wait for an elevator if you were only going to the fifth floor. It's not just that she won't wait for elevators, which she really believes are only provided for the aged and infirm. I have known her to reproach herself on missing one section of a revolving door. And I well remember a time when we missed a train from New York to Washington. I fully expected her to pick up our suitcases and announce, "Well, darling, the exercise will be good for us."

When I have occasion to mutter about the financial problems of maintaining six children in a large house, Mother is quick to get to the root of the problem. "Remember," she says, "you take cabs a lot." In Mother's opinion, an able-bodied woman is perfectly justified in taking a taxi to the hospital if her labor pains are closer than ten minutes apart.

The youngest daughter of wealthy and indulgent parents, Mother went to finishing schools in France and to the Royal Conservatory of Music in London. Thus, when she came to America to marry my father, her only qualifications for the role of housewife and mother were the ability to speak four languages, play three musical instruments, and make blanc mange. I, naturally, wasn't around during those first troubled months when Mother learned to cook. But my father can still recall the day she boiled corn on the cob, a delicacy unknown in Ireland at that time, for five hours until the cobs were tender. . . . .Mother would cook things she had no intention of eating. Where food is concerned, she is totally conservative. . . .

On the other hand she was always willing to prepare all manner of exotic dishes for Dad and the rest of us. In the old days the men who worked for my father frequently gave him gifts of game—venison, rabbit, and the like. Occasionally we children would protest. I recall becoming quite tearful over the prospect of eating deer, on the theory that it might be Bambi. But Mother was always firm. "Nonsense," she would say, "eat up, it's just like chicken."

But one night she went too far. I don't know where she got this enormous slab of meat; I don't think my father brought it home. It stood overnight in the icebox in some complicated solution of brine and herbs. The next day the four of us were told that we could each invite a friend to dinner. Mother spent most of the day lovingly preparing her roast. That night there were ten of us around the dining room table, and if Mother seemed too busy serving the rest of us to eat anything herself, that was not at all unusual. At this late date I have no impression of what the meat tasted like. But I know that we were all munching away when Mother beamed happily at us and asked, "Well, children, how are you enjoying the bear?"

To the four low-metabolism types she inexplicably produced, Mother's energy has always seemed awesome. "What do you think," she's prone to say, "Do I have time to cut the grass before I stuff the turkey?" But her whirlwind activity is potentially less

dangerous than her occasional moments of repose. Then she sits, staring into space, clearly lost in languorous memories. The faint, fugitive smile that hovers about her lips suggests the gentle melancholy of one hearing Mozart played beautifully. Suddenly, she leaps to her feet. "I know it will work," she says. "All we have to do is remove that wall, plug up the windows, and extend the porch."

It's undoubtedly fortunate that she has the thrust and energy of a well-guided missile. Otherwise, she wouldn't get a lick of work done, because everybody who comes to her house, whether to read the gas meter or collect for UNICEF, always stays at least an hour. I used to think that they were one and all beguiled by her Irish accent. But I have gradually gleaned that they are telling her the story of their invariably unhappy lives. "Do you remember my lovely huckleberry man?" Mother will ask. "Oh, *yes* you do—he had red hair and ears. Well, his brother-in-law sprained his back and hasn't worked in six months, and we're going to have to take a bundle of clothes over to those children." Or, again: "Do you remember that nice girl in the Scranton Dry Goods? Oh, *yes* you do, she was in lamp shades and she had gray hair and wore gray dresses. Well, she's having an operation next month and you must remember to pray for her."

Mother's credo, by the way, is that if you want something, anything, don't just sit there—pray for it. And she combines a Job-like patience in the face of the mysterious ways of the Almighty with a flash of Irish rebellion which will bring her to say—and I'm sure she speaks for many of us— "Jean, what I am really looking for is a blessing that's not in disguise." . . .

The first time I had a collection of short pieces brought out in book form, I sent an advance copy to Mother. She was naturally delighted. Her enthusiasm fairly bubbled off the pages of the letter. "Darling," she wrote, "isn't it marvelous the way those old pieces of yours finally came to the surface like a dead body!"

I knew when I started this that all I could do was list the things Mother says, because it's not possible, really, to describe her. All my life I have heard people break off their lyrical descriptions of Kitty and announce helplessly, "You'll just have to meet her."

However, I recognize, if I cannot describe, the lovely festive air she always brings with her, so that she can arrive any old day in July and suddenly it seems to be Christmas Eve and the children seem handsomer and better behaved and all the adults seem more charming and—

Well, you'll just have to meet her.

All Over

from *Father of the Bride* by Edward Streeter

The last guest had gone. The last damp hand had been wrung. The bridal party had disappeared noisily to seek bigger and newer adventure. The Dunstans had left. The relatives had returned to the oblivion from which they had emerged. Mr. and Mrs. Banks were alone with the wreckage.

They sat limply in two armchairs which Mr. Banks had dragged down from upstairs. The rug was covered with confetti. The few casual tables which Mr. Massoula had left in the living room were garnished with gray rings. Here and there on the white paint of the sills were the dark signatures of cigarettes. The floral background of the reception line obliterated the fireplace. They stared at it in silence.

"She did look lovely in that going-away suit," said Mrs. Banks dreamily. "Didn't you think it was good-looking?"

Mr. Banks couldn't remember it very well. He knew she had had on something tan. There his detail stopped. But her face was etched forever on his memory as she stood on the landing waiting to throw the bride's bouquet.

"She's a darling," he said.

"Queer the Griswolds didn't come," mused Mrs. Banks. "They accepted and Jane told me they were coming."

"I don't see how you know whether they came or not."

"I know everybody that was here and everybody that wasn't," said Mrs. Banks complacently.

Mr. Banks did not question it. This woman who couldn't remember the details of the most elementary problem for five minutes would remember now and forever everyone who came, everyone who didn't— and those who crashed the gate. . . .

In another compartment of Mr. Banks' brain an adding machine was relentlessly at work. The figures came pouring out and each time they were greater than before. . . .

"I suppose," said Mrs. Banks, "we ought to get out the vacuum cleaner and not leave this whole mess for Delilah tomorrow. I'll go up and change my dress."

Mr. Banks followed her upstairs glumly. Like a fog blowing in from the sea, he could feel the first wisps of depression fingering into his soul.

Here was the place where she had stood. He paused and looked over the rail at the confetti-strewn hall. Queer about places and houses. They remained the same yet they were never the same. By no stretch of the imagination was this the same spot from which Kay had tossed her flowers to the waving arms below.

He continued upstairs, thinking of all the money and energy that was wasted each year visiting the scenes of great events under the impression that they were still the same places.

At the door to the spare room where the presents were on display, he paused, then lit the light and went in. This morning it had been a gay, exciting place, full of anticipation and promise of things to come. The animating spirit was gone. Now it was just a bare room with card tables along the walls covered with china and glassware. It was as impersonal as a store.

He tried to shake off the cloud that was settling over him. In the bathroom a single bottle of champagne rested quietly in the wash basin. It had been put there by someone just before Mr. Massoula ran out. Heaven knew what for. It was still cold. For a moment he debated whether to open it. Then he turned, went downstairs, and got

AMERICAN FAMILY TREASURY

out the vacuum cleaner.

An hour later the last particle of confetti had been transformed to the bulging back of the machine. They sat once more in the chairs in the living room gazing with exhausted faces at the banked greens in front of the fireplace. . . .

He went quietly up to the bathroom and drew the cork in the last remaining bottle. From the spare room he selected two of Kay's new champagne glasses and returned to his wife.

Carefully he filled two glasses and handed one to Mrs. Banks. Behind the floral background the clock on the mantle struck twelve. The whistle of a train from the city hooted in the distance as it rounded the curve into the Fairview Manor station. A dog was barking somewhere.

"How," said Mr. Banks raising his glass.

"How," said Mrs. Banks.

Toys and Games

The first baseball cards appeared in 1880. Before their legendary pairing with bubble gum, the cards were found inside cigarette packages.

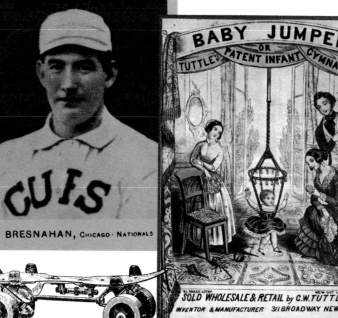

BRESNAHAN, Chicago - Nationals

BABY JUMPER.
OR
TUTTLE'S PATENT INFANT GYMNASIUM.

SOLD WHOLESALE & RETAIL by C.W.TUTTLE
INVENTOR & MANUFACTURER 311 BROADWAY NEW YORK

Lionel Manufacturing Company built the first toy trains in 1900 in New York City. The trains were not originally marketed as toys, but as novelty items for store window displays. Window shoppers ignored the other merchandise, however, and asked about the trains, beginning an American obsession with miniature railroad sets that remains strong today.

Mr. Potato Head was the first toy advertised on television, making his debut on May 1, 1952. The toy was originally sold as a collection of plastic face pieces to be attached to a real potato. The plastic potato head appeared in 1964 in response to parents' complaints about the dangerously sharp tips needed on eyes, noses, and mouths to puncture real potato skin.

1883, 16-year-old George S. Parker of
lem, Mass., invented a game he called
NKING. At the encouragement of
ends, he took the game to the large
ston publishers. Parker met with re-
ction all round; undaunted,
formed his own small com-
ny and successfully market-
his game. That company,
er called Parker Brothers,
mains in the game business
day after more than 100 years.

he game MONOPOLY was
vented by Charles B. Darrow of
ermantown, Pennsylvania.
arker Brothers originally turned
own Darrow's game, telling
im that it took too long to play,
as overly complicated, and had
52 fundamental playing errors."

In 1912, two-thirds of toy sales came
at Christmas and many stores carried
no toys at all during the remainder of
the year. By 1920, however, toy
sales had tripled, and parents had
begun to buy toys for their children
year round.

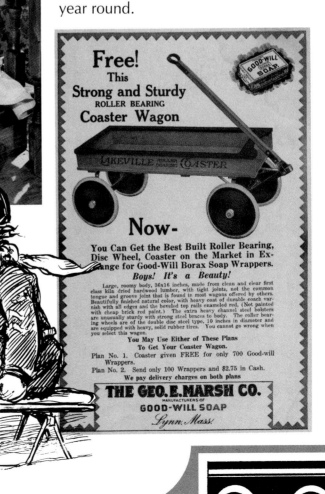

Free!
This
Strong and Sturdy
ROLLER BEARING
Coaster Wagon

GOOD-WILL SOAP

Now-

You Can Get the Best Built Roller Bearing,
Disc Wheel, Coaster on the Market in Ex-
ange for Good-Will Borax Soap Wrappers.
Boys! It's a Beauty!

Large, roomy body, 36x16 inches, made from clean and clear first
class kiln dried hardwood lumber, with tight joints, not the common
tongue and groove joint that is found in most wagons offered by others.
Beautifully finished natural color, with heavy coat of durable coach var-
nish with all edges and the beveled top rails enameled red. (Not painted
with cheap brick red paint.) The extra heavy channel steel bolsters
are unusually sturdy with strong steel braces to body. The roller bear-
ing wheels are of the double disc steel type, 10 inches in diameter and
are equipped with heavy, solid rubber tires. You cannot go wrong when
you select this wagon.

**You May Use Either of These Plans
To Get Your Coaster Wagon.**

Plan No. 1. Coaster given FREE for only 700 Good-will
Wrappers.
Plan No. 2. Send only 100 Wrappers and $2.75 in Cash.
We pay delivery charges on both plans

THE GEO. E. MARSH CO.
MANUFACTURERS OF
GOOD-WILL SOAP
Lynn, Mass.

MONOPOLY

MONOPOLY

THE FAMILY IN POETRY

Francine & Louise
1908

On the beach with
Paula the Poet
1908

Paul age 5

Dressed in Sunday best
Christmas 1907

Mildred's favorite chair.
She loved rhymes.

Off on a Sunday drive

The Old Oaken Bucket

How dear to my heart are the scenes of my childhood,
When fond recollection presents them to view!
The orchard, the meadow, the deep, tangled wildwood,
And every loved spot which my infancy knew,
The wide-spreading pond and the mill that stood by it,
The bridge and the rock where the cataract fell;
The cot of my father, the dairy house nigh it,
And even the rude bucket that hung in the well.

That moss-covered bucket I hailed as a treasure,
For often at noon when returned from the field,
I found it the source of an exquisite pleasure,
The purest and sweetest that nature can yield.
How ardent I seized it, with hands that were glowing,
And quick to the white-pebbled bottom it fell.
Then soon, with the emblem of truth overflowing,
And dripping with coolness it fell from the well.

How sweet from the green, mossy brim to receive it,
As, poised on the curb, it inclined to my lips!
Not a full, blushing goblet could tempt me to leave it,
Though filled with the nectar that Jupiter sips.
And now, far removed from the loved habitation,
The tear of regret will intrusively swell,
As fancy reverts to my father's plantation,
And sighs for the bucket that hung in the well.

Samuel Woodworth

Playtime

When the voices of children are heard on the green
And laughing is heard on the hill,
My heart is at rest within my breast,
And everything else is still.

"Then come home, my children, the sun is gone down,
And the dews of night arise;
Come, come, leave off play, and let us away
Till the morning appears in the skies."

"No, no, let us play, for it is yet day,
And we cannot go to sleep;
Besides in the sky the little birds fly,
And the hills are covered with sheep."

William Blake

AMERICAN FAMILY TREASURY

Our Silly Little Sister

To begin with she wouldn't have fallen in
If she hadn't been acting so silly.
First thing we saw was her hair ribbon there
On top like a water lily.

In less than a minute we'd gotten her out
And set her down quickly to drain,
And do you know what she said
through her dripping hair?
"I want to go swimming again."

"Swimming?" we cried.
"Do you think *you* can swim?"
She sat there so scowly and black.
"*Much better than you can,
besides I don't care!*"
We couldn't think what to say back.

Dorothy Aldis

THE FAMILY IN POETRY

Father

We all look on with anxious eyes,
When Father carves the duck,
And Mother almost always sighs,
When Father carves the duck.
Then all of us prepare to rise,
And hold our bibs before our eyes,
And be prepared for some surprise,
When Father carves the duck.

He braces up and grabs a fork
Whene'er he carves the duck,
And won't allow a soul to talk,
Until he's carved the duck.
The fork is jabbed into the sides,
Across the breast the knife he slides,
While every careful person hides
From flying chips of duck.

The platter's always sure to slip
When Father carves the duck,
And how it makes the dishes skip!
Potatoes fly amuck!
The squash and cabbage leap in space,
We get some gravy in our face,
And Father mutters Hindu grace
Whene'er he carves a duck.

We then have learned to walk around
The dining room and pluck
From off the windowsills and walls
Our share of Father's duck.
While Father growls and blows and jaws,
And swears the knife was full of flaws,
And Mother jeers at him because
He couldn't carve a duck.

Ernest Vincent Wright

THE FAMILY IN POETRY

A Perfect Night

On a cozy winter evening
In the lamplight's gentle glow,
We sit around the fireplace,
Snug and safe from the cold and snow.

We pop some corn and read awhile
As snow falls gently down.
It covers every field and stream
And everything in town.

We share a sense of oneness
That never seems to cease;
A special sort of closeness
Of comfort and of peace.

As we spend a family evening
Close beside the flickering light
I am so thankful to our Lord
For such a perfect night.

Thelma Hice Moeller

The Children's Hour

Between the dark and the daylight,
When the night is beginning to lower,
Comes a pause in the day's occupations
That is known as the Children's Hour.

I hear in the chamber above me
The patter of little feet,
The sound of a door that is opened,
And voices soft and sweet.

From my study I see in the lamplight,
Descending the broad hall stair,
Grave Alice, and laughing Allegra,
And Edith with golden hair.

A whisper, and then a silence:
Yet I know by their merry eyes
They are plotting and planning together
To take me by surprise.

A sudden rush from the stairway,
A sudden raid from the hall!
By three doors left unguarded
They enter my castle wall!

They climb up into my turret
O'er the arms and back of my chair;
If I try to escape they surround me;
They seem to be everywhere.

They almost devour me with kisses,
Their arms about me entwine,
Till I think of the Bishop of Bingen
In his Mouse-Tower on the Rhine!

Do you think, O blue-eyed banditti,
Because you have scaled the wall,
Such an old mustache as I am
Is not a match for you all?

I have you fast in my fortress,
And will not let you depart,
But put you down in the dungeon
In the round-tower of my heart.

And there I will keep you forever,
Yes, forever and a day,
Till the wall shall crumble to ruin,
And molder in dust away.

Henry Wadsworth Longfellow

THE FAMILY IN POETRY

The Reading Mother

I had a Mother who read to me
Sagas of pirates who scoured the sea,
Cutlasses clenched in their yellow teeth,
"Blackbirds" stowed in the hold beneath.

I had a Mother who read me lays
Of ancient and gallant and golden days;
Stories of Marmion and Ivanhoe,
Which every boy has a right to know.

I had a Mother who read me tales
Of Gelert the hound of the hills of Wales,
True to his trust till his tragic death,
Faithfulness blent with his final breath.

I had a Mother who read me the things
That wholesome life to the boy heart brings—
Stories that stir with an upward touch,
Oh, that each mother of boys were such!

You may have tangible wealth untold;
Caskets of jewels and coffers of gold.
Richer than I you can never be—
I had a Mother who read to me.

Strickland Gillilan

AMERICAN FAMILY TREASURY

THE FAMILY IN POETRY

What a Baby Costs

"How much do babies cost?" said he
The other night upon my knee;
And then I said: "They cost a lot;
A lot of watching by a cot,
A lot of sleepless hours and care,
A lot of heart ache and despair,
A lot of fear and trying dread,
And sometimes many tears are shed
In payment for our babies small,
But every one is worth it all.

"For babies people have to pay
A heavy price from day to day—
There is no way to get one cheap.
Why sometimes when they're fast asleep
You have to get up in the night
And go to see that they're all right.
But what they cost in constant care
And worry, does not half compare
With what they bring of joy and bliss—
You'd pay much more for just a kiss.

"Who buys a baby has to pay
A portion of the bill each day;
He has to give his time and thought
Unto the little one he's bought.
He has to stand a lot of pain
Inside his heart and not complain;
And pay with lonely days and sad
For all the happy hours he's had.
All this is what a baby costs, and yet
His smile is worth it all, you bet."

Edgar A. Guest

THE FAMILY IN POETRY

Some Time

Last night, my darling, as you slept,
I thought I heard you sigh,
And to your little crib I crept,
And watched a space thereby;
Then, bending down, I kissed your brow—
For, oh! I love you so—
You are too young to know it now,
But some time you shall know.

Some time, when in a darkened place
Where others come to weep,
Your eyes shall see a weary face
Calm in eternal sleep;
The speechless lips, the wrinkled brow,
The patient smile may show—
You are too young to know it now,
But some time you shall know.

Look backward, then, into the years,
And see me here tonight—
See, O my darling! how my tears
Are falling as I write;
And feel once more upon your brow
The kiss of long ago—
You are too young to know it now,
But some time you shall know.

Eugene Field

AMERICAN FAMILY TREASURY

A Lesson for Mamma

Dear Mamma, if you could just be
A tiny little girl like me,
And I your mamma, you would see
How nice I'd be to you.
I'd always let you have your way;
I'd never frown at you and say,
"You're behaving ill today,
Such conduct will not do."

I'd always give you jelly-cake
For breakfast, and I'd never shake
My head and say, "You must not take
So very large a slice."
I'd never say, "My dear, I trust
You will not make me say you *must*
Eat up your oatmeal"; or "The crust
You'll find, is very nice."

I'd buy you candy every day;
I'd go downtown with you, and say,
"What would my darling like? You may
Have anything you see."
I'd never say, "My pet, you know
'Tis bad for health and teeth, and so
I cannot let you have it. No—
It would be wrong in me."

And every day I'd let you wear
Your nicest dress, and never care
If it should get a great big tear;
I'd only say to you,
"My precious treasure, never mind,
For little clothes *will* tear, I find."
Now, Mamma, wouldn't that be kind?
That's just what *I* should do.

I'd never say, "Well, just a few!"
I'd let you stop your lessons too;
I'd say, "They are too hard for you,
Poor child, to understand."
I'd put the books and slates away;
You shouldn't have a thing but play,
And have a party every day.
A-h-h! wouldn't that be grand!

But, Mamma dear, you cannot grow
Into a little girl, you know,
And I can't be your mamma; so
The only thing to do,
Is just for you to try and see
How very, very nice 'twould be
For *you* to do all this for *me*,
Now Mamma, *couldn't* you?

Sydney Dayre

THE FAMILY IN POETRY

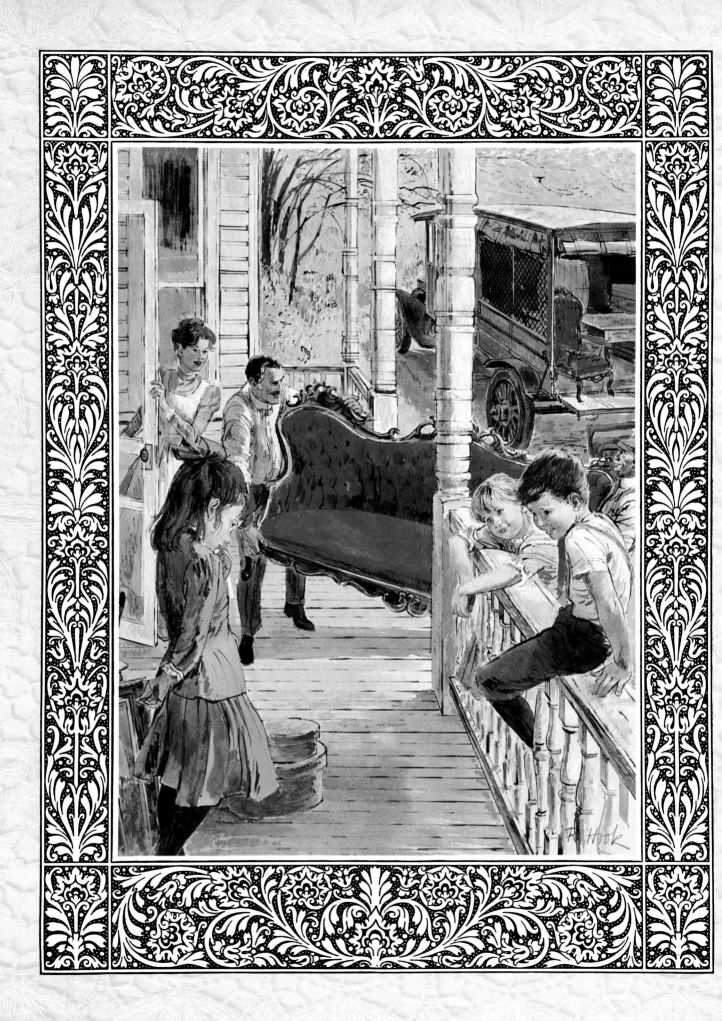

A Prayer for a Little Home

God send us a little home,
To come back to, when we roam.

Low walls and fluted tiles,
Wide windows, a view for miles.

Red firelight and deep chairs,
Small white beds upstairs—

Great talk in little nooks,
Dim colors, rows of books.

One picture on each wall,
Not many things at all.

God send us a little ground,
Tall trees stand around.

Homely flowers in brown sod,
Overhead, thy stars, O God.

God bless Thee, when winds blow,
Our home, and all we know.

Florence Bone

THE FAMILY IN POETRY

Candies and Confections

In 1906 Frank Henry Fleer developed Blibber-Blubber bubble gum. The gum caught the public's interest, but it was too sticky and too brittle for mass popularity. Twenty-two years later, Fleer's son-in-law discovered a way to make the gum non-stick and more flexible. He added pink food coloring and called his new gum Dubble Bubble. The gum was the success Frank Fleer had dreamed about, quickly replacing Tootsie Rolls as the most popular 1-cent confection.

ADAMS CALIFORNIA FRUIT CHEWING GUM
WITH THE FRUITY FLAVOR

RUTH ROLAND says: Ripe, red cherries and Adams California Fruit Gum I think are equally delicious. I love them both.

Bazooka Bubble Gum came on the market after World War I. It was made by the Topps Company, famous also for its baseball cards.

The OH HENRY bar got its name in a peculiar way. In the Chicago candy store where the bar was invented, a young man named Henry was a frequent visitor of the female clerks, who were constantly asking him to help with odd jobs. When names for a new candy bar were discussed, a salesman remarked that all he ever heard around the store was the phrase "Oh Henry!" and the new candy bar had its name.

The BUTTERFINGER was another candy bar introduced in the '20s. Its name was the result of a public contest, the winning term being a common name given by radio sportscasters to clumsy athletes.

Milk Duds were introduced to American children in 1926 by Chicago candy-maker Milton Holloway. The unusual name was chosen by Mr. Holloway, who set out to create perfectly round candies, but got only "duds."

Cracker Jacks were invented by two German immigrant brothers in Chicago in 1893. The brothers, who sold both candy and popcorn, devised the first version of their now-famous confection for the 1893 Chicago Colombian Exposition. The brothers eventually perfected the sweet popcorn treat, immortalized in the 1908 song "Take Me Out to the Ballgame." It was not until 1912 that each box of Cracker Jacks began concealing a prize.

In 1939, the United States led the world in candy production, making 2 billion pounds per year. Such great quantities were needed to feed the great American appetite for sweets. In that same year, the average American citizen consumed 16 pounds of chocolate and other confections.

AND ALL THE REST OF US

THE flavors imparted by Mother Nature to her products are the most pleasing to the palate. That is one reason why

BAKER'S BREAKFAST COCOA

is universally liked, because it has the *natural flavor* of high grade cocoa beans. No chemicals are used in its manufacture. One never tires of it.

MADE ONLY BY

WALTER BAKER & CO. LTD.
Established 1780   DORCHESTER, MASS.

Booklet of Choice Recipes sent free upon request

SAILOR JACK and CRACKER JACK are registered trademarks and are used with the permission of Borden, Inc.

The BABY RUTH candy bar was the original product of Curtiss Candy Company, founded by a young Chicago salesman named Otto Schnering. It was originally called "Kandy Kake" but in 1921 was improved and renamed, supposedly after President Grover Cleveland's young daughter Ruth. Some insist, however, that the bar was named after baseball star George Herman "Babe" Ruth.

STORYBOOK FAMILIES

Summertime fun
Joan 1909

Betty's Baptism

Good little boys.

Colin + June
learning to read?

Harriet 1911

1910
Dad used to read the
most marvelous bedtime stories

Summertime

from *Little House in the Big Woods* by Laura Ingalls Wilder

Now it was summertime, and people went visiting. Sometimes Uncle Henry, or Uncle George, or Grandpa, came riding out of the Big Woods to see Pa. Ma would come to the door and ask how all the folks were, and she would say:

"Charles is in the clearing."

Then she would cook more dinner than usual, and dinnertime would be longer. Pa and Ma and the visitor would sit talking a little while before they went back to work.

Sometimes Ma let Laura and Mary go across the road and down the hill, to see Mrs. Peterson. The Petersons had just moved in. Their house was new, and always very neat, because Mrs. Peterson had no little girls to muss it up. She was a Swede, and she let Laura and Mary look at the pretty things she had brought from Sweden—laces, and colored embroideries, and china.

Mrs. Peterson talked Swedish to them, and they talked English to her, and they understood each other perfectly. She always gave them each a cookie when they left, and they nibbled the cookies very slowly while they walked home.

Laura nibbled away exactly half of hers, and Mary nibbled exactly half of hers, and the other halves they saved for Baby Carrie. Then when they got home, Carrie had two half cookies, and that was a whole cookie.

This wasn't right. All they wanted to do was divide the cookies fairly with Carrie. Still, if Mary saved half her cookie, while Laura ate the whole of hers, or if Laura saved half, and Mary ate her whole cookie, that wouldn't be fair, either.

They didn't know what to do. So each saved half, and gave it to Baby Carrie. But they always felt that somehow that wasn't quite fair.

Sometimes a neighbor sent word that the entire family was coming to spend the day. Then Ma did extra cleaning and cooking, and opened the package of store sugar. And on the day set, a wagon would come driving up to the gate in the morning and there would be strange children to play with.

When Mr. and Mrs. Huleatt came, they brought Eva and Clarence with them. Eva was a pretty girl, with dark eyes and black curls. She played carefully and kept her dress clean and smooth. Mary liked that, but Laura liked better to play with Clarence.

Clarence was red-headed and freckled, and always laughing. His clothes were pretty, too. He wore a blue suit buttoned all the way up the front with bright, gilt buttons, and trimmed with braid, and he had copper-toed shoes.

The strips of copper across the toes were so glittering bright that Laura wished she were a boy. Little girls didn't wear copper-toes.

Laura and Clarence ran and shouted and climbed trees while Mary and Eva walked nicely together and talked. Ma and Mrs. Huleatt visited and looked at *Godey's Lady's Book* which Mrs. Huleatt had brought, and Pa and Mr. Huleatt looked at the horses and the crops and smoked their pipes.

Once Aunt Lotty came to spend the day. That morning Laura had to stand still a long time while Ma unwound her hair from the cloth strings and combed it into long curls. Mary was all ready, sitting primly on a chair, with her golden curls shining and her china-blue dress fresh and crisp.

Laura liked her own red dress. But Ma pulled her hair dreadfully, and it was brown

John Walter

instead of golden, so that no one noticed it. Everyone noticed and admired Mary's.

"There!" Ma said at last. "Your hair is curled beautifully, and Lotty is coming. Run meet her, both of you, and ask her which she likes best, brown curls or golden curls."

Laura and Mary ran out of the door and down the path, for Aunt Lotty was already at the gate. Aunt Lotty was a big girl, much taller than Mary. Her dress was a beautiful pink and she was swinging a pink sunbonnet by one string.

"Which do you like best, Aunt Lotty," Mary asked, "brown curls, or golden curls?" Ma had told them to ask that, and Mary was a very good little girl who always did exactly as she was told.

Laura waited to hear what Aunt Lotty would say, and she felt miserable.

"I like both kinds best," Aunt Lotty said, smiling. She took Laura and Mary by the hand, one on either side, and they danced along to the door where Ma stood.

The sunshine came streaming through the windows into the house, and everything was so neat and pretty. The table was covered with a red cloth, and the cookstove was polished shining black. Through the bedroom door Laura could see the trundle bed in its place under the big bed. The pantry door stood wide open, giving the sight and smell of goodies on the shelves, and Black Susan came purring down the stairs from the attic, where she had been taking a nap.

It was all so pleasant, and Laura felt so gay and good that no one would ever have thought she could be as naughty as she was that evening.

Aunt Lotty had gone, and Laura and Mary were tired and cross. They were at the woodpile, gathering a pan of chips to kindle the fire in the morning. They always hated to pick up chips, but every day they had to do it. Tonight they hated it more than ever.

Laura grabbed the biggest chip, and Mary said:

"Aunt Lotty likes my hair best, anyway. Golden hair is lots prettier than brown."

Laura's throat swelled tight, and she could not speak. She knew golden hair was prettier than brown. She couldn't speak, so she reached out quickly and slapped Mary's face.

Then she heard Pa say, "Come here, Laura."

She went slowly, dragging her feet. Pa was sitting just inside the door. He had seen her slap Mary.

"You remember," Pa said, "I told you girls you must never strike each other."

Laura began, "But Mary said—"

"That makes no difference," said Pa. "It is what I say that you must mind."

Then he took down a strap from the wall, and he whipped Laura with the strap.

Laura sat on a chair in the corner and sobbed. When she stopped sobbing, she sulked. The only thing in the whole world to be glad about was that Mary had to fill the chip pan all by herself.

At last, when it was getting dark, Pa said again, "Come here, Laura." His voice was kind, and when Laura came he took her on his knee and hugged her close. She sat in the crook of his arm, her head against his shoulder and his long brown whiskers partly covering her eyes, and everything was all right again.

She told Pa all about it, and she asked him, "You don't like golden hair better than brown, do you?"

Pa's blue eyes shone down at her, and he said, "Well, Laura, my hair is brown."

She had not thought of that. Pa's hair was brown, and his whiskers were brown, and she thought brown was a lovely color. But she was glad that Mary had to gather all the chips.

Mrs. Peterkin's Tea-Party

Lucretia Hale

It was important to have a tea-party, as they had all been invited by everybody—the Bromwiches, the Tremletts, and the Gibbonses. It would be such a good chance to pay off some of their old debts, now that the lady from Philadelphia was back again, and her two daughters, who would be sure to make it go off well.

But as soon as they began to make out the list, they saw there were too many to have at once, for there were but twelve cups and saucers in the best set.

"There are seven of us to begin with," said Mr. Peterkin.

"We need not all drink tea," said Mrs. Peterkin.

"I never do," said Solomon John. The little boys never did.

"And we could have coffee, too," suggested Elizabeth Eliza.

"That would take as many cups," observed Agamemnon.

"We could use the everyday set for the coffee," answered Elizabeth Eliza; "they are the right shape. Besides," she went on, "they would not all come. Mr. and Mrs. Bromwich, for instance; they never go out."

"There are but six cups in the everyday set," said Mrs. Peterkin.

The little boys said there were plenty of saucers; and Mr. Peterkin agreed with Elizabeth Eliza that not all would come. Old Mr. Jeffers never went out.

"There are three of the Tremletts," said Elizabeth Eliza; "they never go out together. One of them, if not two, will be sure to have a headache. Ann Maria Bromwich would come, and the three Gibbons boys, and their sister Juliana; but the other sisters are out West, and there is but one Osborne."

It really did seem safe to ask "everybody." They would be sorry, after it was over, that they had not asked more.

"We have the cow," said Mrs. Peterkin, "so there will be as much cream and milk as we shall need."

"And our own pig," said Agamemnon. "I am glad we had it salted; so we can have plenty of sandwiches."

"I will buy a chest of tea," exclaimed Mr. Peterkin. "I have been thinking of a chest for some time."

Mrs. Peterkin thought a whole chest would not be needed; it was as well to buy the tea and coffee by the pound. But Mr. Peterkin determined on a chest of tea and a bag of coffee.

So they decided to give the invitations to all. It might be a stormy evening, and some would be prevented.

The lady from Philadelphia and her daughters accepted.

And it turned out a fair day, and more came than were expected. Ann Maria Bromwich had a friend staying with her, and brought her over, for the Bromwiches were opposite neighbors. And the Tremletts had a niece, and Mary Osborne an aunt, that they took the liberty to bring. . . .

The three Tremletts all came with their niece. They had all had their headaches the day before, and were having that banged feeling you always have after a headache; so they all sat at the same side of the room on the long sofa.

All the Jefferses came, though they had sent uncertain answer. Old Mr. Jeffers had to be helped in with his cane, by Mr. Peterkin.

The Gibbons boys came, and would stand just outside the parlor door. And

Juliana appeared afterward, with the two other sisters, unexpectedly home from the West.

"Got home this morning!" they said. "And so glad to be in time to see everybody—a little tired, to be sure, after forty-eight hours in a sleeping car!"

"Forty-eight!" repeated Mr. Peterkin; and wondered if there were forty-eight people, and why they were all so glad to come, and whether all could sit down.

Old Mr. and Mrs. Bromwich came. They thought it would not be neighborly to stay away. They insisted on getting into the most uncomfortable seats.

Yet there seemed to be seats enough while the Gibbons boys preferred to stand. But they never could sit around a tea-table. Elizabeth Eliza had thought they all might have room at the table, and Solomon John and the little boys could help in the waiting.

It was a great moment when the lady from Philadelphia arrived with her daughters. Mr. Peterkin was talking to Mr. Bromwich, who was a little deaf. The Gibbons boys retreated a little farther behind the parlor door. Mrs. Peterkin hastened forward to shake hands with the lady from Philadelphia, saying:

"Four Gibbons girls and Mary Osborne's aunt,—that makes nineteen; and now—"

It made no difference what she said; for there was such a murmuring of talk, that any words suited. And the lady from Philadelphia wanted to be introduced to the Bromwiches.

"Oh dear, no!" answered Elizabeth Eliza.

Mrs. Peterkin found time to meet Elizabeth Eliza in the side entry and ask if there were going to be cups enough.

"I have set Agamemnon in the front entry to count," said Elizabeth Eliza, putting her hand to her head.

The little boys came to say that the Maberlys were coming.

"The Maberlys!" exclaimed Elizabeth Eliza, "I never asked them."

"It's your father's doing," cried Mrs. Peterkin. "I do believe he asked everybody he saw!" And she hurried back to her guests.

"What if father really has asked everybody!" Elizabeth Eliza said to herself pressing her head again with her hand.

There was the cow and the pig. But if they all took tea or coffee, or both, the cups would not go round.

Agamemnon returned in the midst of her agony.

He had not been able to count the guests, they moved about so, they talked so; and it would not look well to appear to count.

"What shall we do?" exclaimed Elizabeth Eliza.

"We are not a family for an emergency," sighed Agamemnon.

"What do you suppose they do in Philadelphia at the Exhibition, when there are more people than cups and saucers?" asked Elizabeth Eliza. "Could you not go and inquire? I know the lady from Philadelphia is talking about the Exhibition, and telling why she must go back to receive friends. And they must have trouble there! Could you not go in and ask, just as if you wanted to know?"

Agamemnon looked into the room, but there were too many talking to the lady from Philadelphia.

"If we could only look into some book," he said, "The encyclopedia or the dictionary—they are such a help sometimes!"

At this moment he thought of his *Great Triumphs of Great Men*, that he was reading just now. He had not reached the lives of the Stephensons, or any of the men of modern times. He might skip over to them–he knew they were men for emergencies.

He ran up to his room, and met Solomon John coming down with chairs.

"That is a good thought," said Agamem-

non. "I will bring down more upstairs chairs."

"No," said Solomon John, "here are all that can come down; the rest of the bedroom chairs match bureaus, and they never will do!"

Agamemnon kept on to his own room, to consult his books . . . when he was interrupted by the little boys, who came to tell him that Elizabeth Eliza wanted him.

The little boys had been busy thinking. They proposed that the tea-table, with all the things on, should be pushed into the front room, where the company were; and those could take cups who could find cups.

But Elizabeth Eliza feared it would not be safe to push so large a table; it might upset and break what china they had.

Agamemnon came down to find her pouring out tea, in the back room. She called

AMERICAN FAMILY TREASURY

to him:

"Agamemnon, you must bring Mary Osborne to help, and perhaps one of the Gibbons boys would carry round some of the cups."

And so she began to pour out and to send round the sandwiches, and the tea, and the coffee. Let things go as far as they would!

The little boys took the sugar and the cream.

"As soon as they have done drinking, bring back the cups and saucers to be washed," she said to the Gibbons boys and the little boys.

This was an idea of Mary Osborne's.

But what was their surprise, that the more they poured out, the more cups they seemed to have! Elizabeth Eliza took the coffee, and Mary Osborne the tea. Amanda brought fresh cups from the kitchen.

"I can't seem to understand it," Elizabeth Eliza said to Amanda. "Do they come back to you, round through the piazza? Surely there are more cups than there were!"

Her surprise was greater when some of them proved to be coffee cups that matched the set! And they never had had coffee cups.

Solomon John came in at this moment, breathless with triumph.

"Solomon John!" Elizabeth Eliza exclaimed, "I cannot understand the cups!"

"It is my doing," said Solomon John, with an elevated air. "I went to the lady from Philadelphia, in the midst of her talk. 'What do you do in Philadelphia when you haven't enough cups?' 'Borrow of my neighbors,' she answered, as quick as she could."

"She must have guessed," interrupted Elizabeth Eliza.

"That may be," said Solomon John. "But I whispered to Ann Maria Bromwich—she was standing by—and she took me straight over into their closet, and old Mr. Bromwich bought this set, just where we bought ours. And they had a coffee set, too—"

"You mean where mother and father bought them. We were not born," said Elizabeth Eliza.

"It is all the same," said Solomon John. "They match exactly."

So they did, and more and more came in.

Elizabeth Eliza exclaimed:

"And Agamemnon says we are not a family for emergencies!"

"Ann Maria was very good about it," said Solomon John; "and quick, too. And old Mrs. Bromwich has kept all her set of two dozen coffee and tea cups!"

Elizabeth Eliza was ready to faint with delight and relief. She told the Gibbons boys, by mistake, instead of Agamemnon and the little boys. She almost let fall the cups and saucers she took in her hand.

"No trouble now!"

She thought of the cow, and she thought of the pig, and she poured on.

No trouble, except about the chairs. She looked into the room—all seemed to be sitting down, even mother. No, her father was standing, talking to Mr. Jeffers. But he was drinking coffee, and the Gibbons boys were handing around things.

The daughters of the lady from Philadelphia were sitting on shawls on the edge of the window that opened upon the piazza. It was a soft, warm evening, and some of the young people were on the piazza. Everybody was talking and laughing, except those who were listening.

Mr. Peterkin broke away, to bring back his cup and another for more coffee.

"It's a great success, Elizabeth Eliza," he whispered. "The coffee is admirable, and plenty of cups. We asked none too many. I should not mind having a tea party every week."

Elizabeth Eliza sighed with relief as she filled his cup. It was going off well. There were cups enough, but she was not sure she could live over another such hour of anxiety; and what was to be done after tea?

A Home View

from *Five Little Peppers and How They Grew* by Margaret Sidney

The little old kitchen had quieted down from the bustle and confusion of midday; and now, with its afternoon manners on, presented a holiday aspect that, as the principal room in the brown house, it was eminently proper it should have. It was just on the edge of the twilight; and the little Peppers, all except Ben, the oldest of the flock, were taking a "breathing spell" as their mother called it, which meant some quiet work suitable for the hour. It was all the "breathing spell" they could remember, however, poor things; for times were hard with them now. The father had died when Phronsie was a baby, and since then Mrs. Pepper had had hard work to scrape together money enough to put bread into her children's mouths, and to pay the rent of the Little Brown House.

But she had met life too bravely to be beaten down now. So with a stout heart and a cheery face, she had worked away day after day at making coats, and tailoring and mending of all descriptions; and she had seen with pride that couldn't be concealed, her noisy, happy brood growing up around her, and filling her heart with comfort, and making the Little Brown House fairly ring with jollity and fun.

"Poor things!" she would say to herself, "they haven't had any bringing up; they've just scrambled up!" And then she would set her lips together tightly, and fly at her work faster than ever. "I must get learning for 'em some way, but I don't see *how*!"

Once or twice she had thought, "Now the time's coming!" but it never did: for winter shut in very cold, and it took so much more to feed and warm them that the money went faster than ever. And then, when the way seemed clear again, the store changed hands, so that for a long time she failed to get her usual supply of slacks and coats to make; and that made sad havoc in the quarters and half-dollars laid up in her nest egg. But –"Well, it must come some time," she would say to herself; "because it must!" And so at it again she would fly, brisker than ever.

"To help mother" was the great ambition of all the children, older and younger; but in Polly's and Ben's souls, the desire grew so overwhelmingly great as to absorb all lesser things. Many and vast were their secret plans, by which they were to astonish her at some future day, which they would only confide—as they did everything else—to one another. For this brother and sister were everything to each other, and stood loyally together through thick and thin.

Polly was ten, and Ben one year older; and the younger three of "the Five Little Peppers," as they were always called, looked up to them with the intensest admiration and love. What they failed to do, *couldn't* very well be done by *anyone*!

"O dear!" exclaimed Polly, as she sat over in the corner by the window, helping her mother pull out basting threads from a coat she had just finished, and giving an impatient twitch to the sleeve, "I do wish we could ever have any light—just as much as we want! . . . I wish we could have–oh! ever an' ever so many candles; as many as we wanted! I'd light them all, so there! and have it light here *one* night, anyway!" . . .

"How many'd you have, Polly?" asked Joel, curiously, laying down his hammer, and her regarding her with the utmost anxiety.

"Oh, two hundred!" said Polly, decidedly. "I'd have two hundred, all in a row!"

"*Two hundred candles!*" echoed Joel, in

AMERICAN FAMILY TREASURY

amazement. "My whockety, what a lot!"

"Don't say such dreadful words, Joel," put in Polly, nervously, stooping to pick up her spool of basting thread that was racing away all by itself; "'tisn't nice."

"'Tisn't worse'n to wish you'd get things you haven't," retorted Joel. "I don't believe you'd light them all at once," he added, incredulously.

"Yes, I would, too!" replied Polly, recklessly; "two hundred of 'em, if I had a chance; all at once, so there, Joey Pepper!"

"Goodness!" said Mrs. Pepper, "you'd have the house afire! Two hundred candles! Who ever heard of such a thing!"

"Would they burn?" asked Phronsie, anxiously, getting up from the floor where she was crouching with David, overseeing Joel nail on the cover of an old box; and going to Polly's side where she awaited her answer patiently.

"Burn?" said Polly. "There, that's done now, mamsie dear!" And she put the coat, with a last little pat, into her mother's lap. "I guess they would, Phronsie pet." And Polly caught up the little girl, and spun round and round the old kitchen until they were both glad to stop.

"Then," said Phronsie, as Polly put her down and stood breathless after her last glorious spin, "I do wish we might, Polly; oh, just this very one minute!" And Phronsie clasped her fat little hands in rapture at the thought.

"Well," said Polly, giving a look up at the old clock in the corner; "goodness me! It's half past five; and 'most time for Ben to come home!"

Away she flew to get supper. . . .

Phronsie still stood just where Polly left her. *Two hundred candles!* Oh! what *could* it mean! She gazed up to the old beams overhead, and around the dingy walls, and to the old black stove with the fire nearly out, and then over everything the kitchen contained, trying to think how it would seem. To have it bright and winsome and warm! to suit Polly—"Oh!" she screamed.

"Goodness!" cried Polly, taking her head out of the old cupboard in the corner, "how you scared me, Phronsie!"

"I don't want any other celebration," said Mrs. Pepper, . . . "I'm rich now, and that's a fact!"

"Would they never go out?" asked the child, gravely, still standing where Polly left her.

"What?" asked Polly, stopping with a dish of cold potatoes in her hand. "What, Phronsie?

"Why, the candles," said the child, "The ever and ever so many pretty lights!"

"O my senses!" cried Polly, with a little laugh, "haven't you forgotten that! Yes—no, that is Phronsie, if we could have 'em at all, we wouldn't *ever* let them go out!"

"Not once?" asked Phronsie, coming up to Polly with a little skip, and nearly upsetting her, potatoes and all—"not once, Polly, truly?"

"No, not forever—an'-ever," said Polly; "take care, Phronsie, there goes a potato; no, we'd keep 'em always!"

"No, you don't want to," said Mrs. Pepper, coming out of the bedroom in time to catch the last words; "they won't be good tomorrow; better to have 'em tonight, Polly."

"Ma'am!" said Polly, setting down her potato dish on the table, and staring at her mother with all her might—"have *what*, mother?"

"Why, the potatoes, to be sure," replied Mrs. Pepper; "didn't you say you better keep 'em child?"

"'Twasn't potatoes—at all," said Polly, with a little gasp; "'twas—O dear me! here's Ben!" for the door opened, and Phronsie, with a scream of delight, bounded into Ben's arms.

"It's just jolly," said Ben, coming in, his chubby face all aglow, and his big blue eyes shining so honest and true; "it's just jolly to

STORYBOOK FAMILIES

get home! Supper ready, Polly?"

"Yes," said Polly; "that is—all but—" and she dashed off for Phronsie's eating-apron.

"Sometime," said Phronsie, with her mouth half-full, when the meal was nearly over, "we're going to be awful rich; we are

Ben, truly!"

"No?" said Ben, affecting the most hearty astonishment; "you don't say so, Chick."

"Yes," said Phronsie, shaking her yellow head very wisely at him, and diving down into her cup of very weak milk and water to see if Polly *had* put any sugar in

AMERICAN FAMILY TREASURY

by mistake—a custom always expectantly observed. "Yes, we are really, Bensie, very dreadful rich!"

I wish we could be rich now, then," said Ben, taking another generous slice of brown bread; "in time for mamsie's birthday," and he cast a sorrowful glance at Polly.

"I know," said Polly; "O dear! if only we *could* celebrate it!"

"I don't want any other celebration," said Mrs. Pepper, beaming on them so that a flash of sunshine seemed to hop right down on the table, "Than to look around on you all; I'm rich now, and that's a fact!"

"Mamsie doesn't mind her five bothers," cried Polly, jumping up and running to hug her mother, thereby producing a like desire in all the others, who immediately left their seats and followed her example.

"Mother's rich enough," ejaculated Mrs. Pepper, her bright black eyes glistening with delight, as the noisy troop filed back to their bread and potatoes; "if we can only keep together, dears, and grow up good, so that the Little Brown House won't be ashamed of us, that's all I ask."

"Well," said Polly, in a burst of confidence to Ben, after the table had been pushed back against the wall, the dishes nicely washed, wiped, and set up neatly in the cupboard, and all traces of the meal cleared away; "I don't care; let's *try* to get a celebration, somehow, for mamsie!"

"How are you going to do it?" asked Ben, who was of a decidedly practical turn of mind . . . .

"I don't know," said Polly; "but we *must* some way."

"Phoh! that's no good," said Ben, disdainfully; then seeing Polly's face, added, kindly, "let's think, though; and p'r'aps there'll be some way."

"Oh, I know," cried Polly, in delight; " I know the very thing, Ben! Let's make her a cake, a big one, you know, and—"

"She'll see you bake it," said Ben; "or else she'll smell it, and that's just as bad."

"No, she won't, either," replied Polly. "Don't you know she's going to help Mrs. Henderson tomorrow; so there!"

"So she is," said Ben; "good for you, Polly, you always think of everything."

"And then," said Polly, with a comfortable little feeling in her heart at Ben's praise, "why can't we have it all out of the way perfectly splendid when she comes home—and beside, Grandma Bascom'll tell me how. You know we've only got brown flour, Ben; I mean to go right over and ask her now."

"Oh, no, you mustn't," cried Ben, catching hold of her arm as she was preparing to fly off. "Mammy'll find out; better wait till tomorrow; and besides, Polly—" and Ben stopped, unwilling to dampen this propitious beginning. "The stove'll act like everything, tomorrow! I know 'twill; then what'll you do!"

"It shan't!" said Polly, running up to look it in the face; "if it does, I'll shake it; the mean old thing!"

The idea of Polly's shaking the lumbering old black affair, sent Ben into such a peal of laughter that it brought all the other children running to the spot; and nothing would do, but they must one and all be told the reason. So Polly and Ben took them into confidence, which so elated them that half an hour after, when long past her bedtime, Phronsie declared, "I'm not going to bed! I want to sit up like Polly!"

"Don't tease her," whispered Polly to Ben, who thought she ought to go; so she sat straight up on her little stool winking like everything to keep awake.

At last, as Polly was in the midst of one of her liveliest sallies, over tumbled Phronsie, a sleepy little heap, right on to the floor.

"I want—to go—to bed!" she said; "take me—Polly!"

"I thought so," laughed Polly, and bundled her off into the bedroom.

Independence Day

Laura Ingalls Wilder

Almanzo was eating breakfast before he remembered that this was the Fourth of July. He felt more cheerful.

It was like Sunday morning. After breakfast he scrubbed his face with soap till it shone, and he parted his wet hair and combed it sleekly down. He put on his sheep's-gray trousers and his shirt of French calico, and his vest and his short round coat. . . .

He put on his round straw hat, which Mother had made of braided oat straw, and he was all dressed up for Independence Day. He felt very fine.

Father's shining horses were hitched to the shining, red-wheeled buggy, and they all drove away in the cool sunshine. All the country had a holiday air. Nobody was working in the fields and along the road the people in their Sunday clothes were driving to town.

Father's swift horses passed them all. They passed by wagons and carts and buggies. They passed gray horses and black horses and dappled-gray horses. Almanzo raised his hat whenever he sailed past anyone he knew, and would have been perfectly happy if only he had been driving that swift, beautiful team.

At the church sheds in Malone he helped Father unhitch. Mother and the girls and Royal hurried away. But Almanzo would rather help with the horses than do anything else. He couldn't drive them, but he could tie their halters and buckle on their blankets, and stroke their soft noses and give them hay.

Then he went out with Father and they walked on the crowded sidewalks. All the stores were closed, but the ladies and gentlemen were walking up and down and talking.

Ruffled little girls carried parasols, and all the boys were dressed up, like Almanzo. Flags were everywhere, and in the square the band was playing "Yankee Doodle." The fifes tooted and the flutes shrilled and the drums came in with a rub-a-dub-dub. . . . Even the grown-ups had to keep time to it. And there, in the corner of the square, were the two brass cannons!

The band stopped playing, and the minister prayed. Then the band tuned up again and everybody rose. Men and boys took off their hats. The band played and everybody sang:

Oh, say, can you see
by the dawn's early light,
What so proudly we hailed
at the twilight's last gleaming, . . .

From the top of the flagpole, up against the blue sky, the Stars and Stripes were fluttering. Everybody looked at the American flag, and Almanzo sang with all his might. . . .

The music was so gay; the bandsmen in their blue and red and their brass buttons tooted merrily, and the fat drummer beat a rat-a-tat-tat on the drum. All the flags were fluttering and everybody was happy, because they were free and independent and this was Independence Day. And it was time to eat dinner.

Almanzo helped father feed the horses while Mother and the girls spread the picnic lunch on the grass in the churchyard. Many others were picnicking there, too, and after he had eaten all that he could, Almanzo went back to the square.

There was a lemonade stand by the hitching posts. A man sold pink lemonade, a nickel a glass, and a crowd of the town boys were standing around him. Cousin Frank was there. Almanzo had a drink at the town

AMERICAN FAMILY TREASURY

pump, but Frank said he was going to buy lemonade. He had a nickel. He walked up to the stand and bought a glass of the pink lemonade and drank it slowly. He smacked his lips and rubbed his stomach and said:

"Mmmmm! Why don't you buy some?"

"Where'd you get the nickel?" Almanzo asked. He had never had a nickel. Father gave him a penny every Sunday to put in the church collection box; he had never had any other money.

"My father gave it to me," Frank bragged. "My father gives me a nickel every time I ask him."

"Well, so would my father if I asked him," said Almanzo.

"Well, why don't you ask him?" Frank did not believe that Father would give Almanzo a nickel. Almanzo did not know whether Father would or not.

"Because I don't want to," he said.

"He wouldn't give you a nickel," Frank said.

"He would, too."

"I dare you to ask him," Frank said. The other boys were listening. Almanzo put his hands in his pockets and said:

"I'd just as lief ask him if I wanted to."

"Yah, you're scared!" Frank jeered. "Double dare! Double dare!"

Father was a little way down the street talking to Mr. Paddock, the wagon-maker. Almanzo walked slowly toward them. He was faint-hearted, but he had to go. The nearer he got to Father, the more he dreaded asking for a nickel. He had never before thought of doing such a thing. He was sure Father would not give it to him.

He waited till father stopped talking and looked at him.

"What is it, son?" Father asked.

Almanzo was scared. "Father," he said.

"Well, son?"

"Father," Almanzo said, "would you—would you give me—a nickel?"

He stood there while Father and Mr. Paddock looked at him, and he wished he could get away. Finally Father asked:

"What for?"

Almanzo looked down at his moccasins and muttered:

"Frank had a nickel. He bought pink lemonade."

"Well," Father said slowly, "if Frank treated you, it's only right you should treat him." Father put his hand in his pocket. Then he stopped and asked:

"Did Frank treat you to lemonade?"

Almanzo wanted so badly to get the nickel that he nodded. Then he squirmed and said:

"No, Father."

Father looked at him a long time. Then he took out his wallet and opened it, and slowly he took out a round, big, silver half-dollar. He asked:

"Almanzo, do you know what this is?"

"Half a dollar," Almanzo answered.

"Yes, but do you know what half a dollar is?"

Almanzo didn't know it was anything but a half a dollar.

"It's work, son," Father said. "That's what money is, it's hard work."

Mr. Paddock chuckled. "The boy's too young, Wilder," he said. "You can't make a youngster understand that."

"Almanzo's smarter than you think," said Father.

Almanzo didn't understand at all. He wished he could get away. But Mr. Paddock was looking at Father just as Frank looked at Almanzo when he double-dared him, and Father had said Almanzo was smart, so Almanzo tried to look like a smart boy. Father asked:

"You know how to raise potatoes, Almanzo?"

"Yes," Almanzo said.

"Say you have seed potato in the spring, what do you do with it?"

"You cut it up," Almanzo said.

"Go on, son."

STORYBOOK FAMILIES

"Then you harrow—first you manure the field, and plow it. Then you harrow and mark the ground. And plant the potatoes, and plow them, and hoe them. You plow and hoe them twice."

"That's right, son. And then?"

"Then you dig them and put them down in the cellar."

"Yes. Then you pick them over all winter; you throw out all the little ones and rotten ones. Come spring, you load them up and haul them here to Malone, and you sell them. And if you get a good price, son, how much do you get to show for all that work? How much do you get for a half bushel of potatoes?"

"Half a dollar," Almanzo said.

"Yes," said Father. "That's what's in this half-dollar, Almanzo. The work that raised half a bushel of potatoes is in it."

Almanzo looked at the round piece of money that Father held up. It looked small, compared with all that work.

"You can have it, Almanzo," Father said. Almanzo could hardly believe his ears. Father gave him the heavy half-dollar.

"It's yours," said Father. "You could buy a suckling pig with it, if you want to. You could raise it, and it would raise a litter of pigs, worth four, five dollars a piece. Or you could trade that half-dollar for lemonade and drink it up. You do as you want, it's your money."

Almanzo forgot to say thank you. He held the half-dollar a minute, then he put his hand in his pocket and went back to the boys by the lemonade stand. The man was calling out,

"Step this way, step this way! Ice-cold lemonade, pink lemonade, only five cents a glass! Only half a dime, ice-cold pink lemonade! The twentieth part of a dollar!"

Frank asked Almanzo:

"Where's the nickel?"

"He didn't give me a nickel," said Almanzo, and Frank yelled:

"Yah, yah! I told you he wouldn't! I told you so!"

AMERICAN FAMILY TREASURY

"He gave me a half a dollar," said Almanzo.

The boys wouldn't believe it till he showed them. Then they crowded about, waiting for him to spend it. He showed it to them all, and put it back in his pocket.

"I'm going to look around," he said, "and buy me a good little suckling pig."

The band came marching down the street, and they all ran along beside it. The flag was gloriously waving in front, then came the buglers blowing and the fifers tootling and the drummer rattling the drumsticks on the drum. Up the street and down the street went the band, with all the boys following it, and then it stopped in the square by the brass cannons. . . .

The cannons sat in their haunches, pointing their long barrels upward. The band kept on playing. Two men kept shouting, "Stand back! Stand back!" and other men were pouring black powder into the cannons' muzzles and pushing it down with wads of cloth on rods.

The iron rods had two handles, and two men pushed and pulled on them, driving the black powder down the brass barrels. Then all the boys ran to pull grass and weeds along the railroad tracks. They carried them by armfuls to the cannons, and then crowded the weeds into the cannons' muzzles and drove them down with the long rods.

A bonfire was burning by the railroad tracks, and long iron rods were heating in it.

When all the weeds and grass had been packed tight against the powder in the cannons, a man took a little more powder in his hand and carefully filled the two little touch-holes in the barrels. Now everybody was shouting. "Stand back! Stand back!"

Mother took hold of Almanzo's arm and made him come away with her.

Two men took the long iron rods from the fire. Everybody was still, watching. Standing as far behind the cannons as they could, the two men stretched out the rods

and touched their red hot tips to the touch-holes. A little flame like a candle flame flickered up from the powder. The little flames stood there burning; nobody breathed. Then—BOOM!

The cannons leaped backward, the air was full of flying grass and weeds. Almanzo ran with all the other boys to feel the warm muzzles of the cannons. . . .

"That's the noise that made the Redcoats run!" Mr. Paddock said to Father.

"Maybe," Father said, tugging his beard. "But it was muskets that won the Revolution. And don't forget it was axes and plows that made the country." . . .

That night when they were going to the house with the milk, Almanzo asked Father, "Father, how was it axes and plows that made this country? Didn't we fight England for it?"

"We fought for Independence, son," Father said. "But all the land our forefathers had was a little strip of country, here between the mountains and the ocean. All the way from here west was Indian country, and Spanish and French, and English country. It was farmers who took all that country and made it America."

"How?" Almanzo asked.

"Well, son, the Spaniards were soldiers, and high-and-mighty gentlemen that only wanted gold. And the French were fur traders, wanting to make quick money. And England was busy fighting wars. But we were farmers, son; we wanted the land. It was farmers that went over the mountains, and cleared the land, and settled it, and farmed it, and hung on to their farms.

"This country goes three thousand miles west now. It goes way out beyond Kansas, and beyond the great American Desert, over mountains bigger than these mountains, and down to the Pacific Ocean. It's the biggest country in the world, and it was farmers who took all that country and made it America, son. Don't you ever forget that."

STORYBOOK FAMILIES

Christmas Every Day

William Dean Howells

The little girl came into her papa's study, as she always did Saturday morning before breakfast, and asked for a story. He tried to beg off that morning, for he was very busy, but she would not let him. So he began:

"Well, once there was a little pig—"

She put her hand over his mouth and stopped him at the word. She said she had heard little pig stories until she was perfectly sick of them.

"Well, what kind of story shall I tell, then?"

"About Christmas. It's getting to be the season. It's past Thanksgiving already."

"It seems to me," argued Papa, "That I have told as often about Christmas as I have about little pigs."

"No difference! Christmas is more interesting."

"Well!" Her papa roused himself from his writing by a great effort. "Well, then, I'll tell you about the little girl that wanted it Christmas every day of the year. How would you like that?"

"First-rate!" said the little girl; and she nestled into a comfortable shape in his lap, ready for listening.

"Very well, then, this little pig—Oh, what are you pounding me for?"

"Because you said little pig instead of little girl."

"I should like to know the difference between a little pig and a little girl who wanted it Christmas every day!"

"Papa," said the little girl warningly, "if you don't go on, I'll give it to you!" And at this her papa darted off like lightning, and began to tell the story as fast as he could. . . .

Well, once there was a little girl who liked Christmas so much that she wanted it to be Christmas every day in the year; and as soon as Thanksgiving was over she began to send postal cards to the old Christmas Fairy to ask if she mightn't have it. But the old Fairy never answered any of the postals; and, after a while, the girl found out that the Fairy was pretty particular and wouldn't notice anything but letters, not even correspondence cards in envelopes; but real letters on sheets of paper, and sealed outside with a monogram—or your initial, anyway. So, then, she began to send her letters; and in about three weeks—or just the day before Christmas, it was—she got a letter from the Fairy saying she might have it Christmas every day for a year, and then they would see about having it longer.

The little girl was a good deal excited already preparing for the old-fashioned, once-a-year Christmas that was coming the next day, and perhaps the Fairy's promise didn't make such an impression on her as it would have at some other time. She just resolved to keep it to herself and surprise everybody with it as it kept coming true; and then it slipped out of her mind altogether.

She had a splendid Christmas. She went to bed early, so as to let Santa Claus have a chance at the stockings, and in the morning she was up the first of anybody and went and felt them, and found hers all lumpy with packages of candy, and oranges and grapes, and pocket-books and rubber balls and all kinds of small presents, and her big brother's with nothing but the tongs in them, and her young lady sister's with a new silk umbrella, and her papa's and mama's with potatoes and pieces of coal wrapped up in tissue paper, just as they always had every Christmas. Then she waited around till the rest of the family were up, and she was the first to

burst into the library, when the doors were opened, and look at the large presents laid out on the library-table—books, and portfolios, and boxes of stationery, and breast-pins, and dolls, and little stoves, and dozens of handkerchiefs, and ink-stands, and skates, and snow-shovels, and photograph frames, and little easels, and boxes of water-colors, and Turkish paste, and nougat, and candied cherries, and dolls' houses, and water-proofs—and the big Christmas tree, lighted and standing in a wastebasket in the middle.

She had a splendid Christmas all day. She ate so much candy that she did not want any breakfast; and the whole forenoon the presents kept pouring in that the expressman had not had time to deliver the night before; and she went round giving the presents she had got for other people, and came home and ate turkey and cranberry for dinner, and plum-pudding and nuts and raisins and oranges and more candy, and then went out and coasted and came in with a stomach ache, crying; and her papa said he would see if his house was turned into that sort of fool's paradise another year; and they had a light supper, and pretty early everybody went to bed cross.

Here the little girl pounded her papa in the back again.

"Well, what now? Did I say pigs?"

"You made them act like pigs."

"Well, didn't they?"

"No matter; you oughtn't to put it into the story."

"Very well, then, I'll take it all out."

Her father went on:

The little girl slept very heavily, and she slept very late, but she was awakened at last by the other children dancing around her bed with their stockings full of presents in their hands.

"What is it?" said the little girl, and she rubbed her eyes and tried to rise up in bed.

"Christmas! Christmas! Christmas!" they all shouted, waving their stockings.

"Nonsense! It was Christmas yesterday."

Her brothers and sisters just laughed. "We don't know about that. It's Christmas today, anyway. You come to the library and see."

Then all at once it flashed on the little girl that the Fairy was keeping her promise, and her year of Christmases was beginning. She was dreadfully sleepy, but she sprang up like a lark—a lark that had overeaten itself and gone to bed cross—and darted into the library. There it was again! Books and portfolios, and boxes of stationery, and breast-pins—

"You needn't go over it all, Papa; I guess I can remember just what was there," said the little girl.

Well, and there was the Christmas tree blazing away, and the family picking out their presents, but looking pretty sleepy, and her father perfectly puzzled, and her mother ready to cry. "I'm sure I don't see how I'm to dispose of all these things," said her mother, and her father said it seemed to him they had something just like it the day before, but he supposed he must have dreamed it. This struck the little girl as the best kind of joke; and so she ate so much candy she didn't want any breakfast, and went round carrying presents, and had turkey and cranberry for dinner, and then went out and coasted, and came in with a—

"Papa!"

"Well, what now?"

"What did you promise, you forgetful thing?"

"Oh! oh, yes!"

Well, the next day, it was just the same thing over and over again, but everybody getting crosser; and at the end of a week's time so many people had lost their tempers that you could pick up lost tempers anywhere; they were perfectly strewed on the ground. Even when people tried to recover their tempers they usually got somebody else's, and it made the most dreadful mix.

STORYBOOK FAMILIES

The little girl began to get frightened, keeping the secret all to herself; she wanted to tell her mother, but she didn't dare to; and she was ashamed to ask the Fairy to take back her gift, it seemed ungrateful and ill-bred, and she thought she would try to stand it, but she hardly knew how she could, for a whole year. So it went on and on, and it was Christmas on St. Valentine's Day, and Washington's Birthday just the same as any day, and it didn't even skip the First of April, though everything was counterfeit that day, and that was some little relief.

After a while, coal and potatoes began to be awfully scarce, so many had been wrapped in tissue paper to fool papas and mammas with. Turkeys got to be about a thousand dollars apiece—

"Papa!"

"You're beginning to fib."

"Well, two thousand, then."

Well, after it had gone on for about three or four months, the little girl, whenever she came into the room in the morning and saw those great ugly lumpy stockings dangling at the fireplace, and the disgusting presents around everywhere, used to just sit down and burst out crying. In six months she was perfectly exhausted; she couldn't even cry anymore; she just lay in the lounge and rolled her eyes and panted. About the beginning of October she took to sitting

AMERICAN FAMILY TREASURY

down on dolls, wherever she found them—French doll, or any kind—she hated the sight of them so; and by Thanksgiving she was crazy, and just slammed her presents across the room.

By that time people didn't carry presents around nicely anymore. They flung them over the fence or through the window, or anything.

"Did I tell you how it was on the Fourth of July?"

"No, how was it?" And the little girl nestled closer, in expectation of something uncommon. . . .

The Fourth of July orations all turned into Christmas carols, and when everybody tried to read the Declaration, instead of saying, "When in the course of human events it becomes necessary," he was sure to sing, "God rest you merry gentlemen." It was perfectly awful.

The little girl drew a deep sigh of satisfaction.

"And how was it at Thanksgiving?" she asked.

Her papa hesitated. "Well, I'm almost afraid to tell you. I'm afraid you'll think it wicked."

"Well, tell, anyway," said the little girl.

Well, before it came Thanksgiving, it had leaked out who had caused all these Christmases. . . . and now, when it came Thanksgiving . . . they said that all the turkeys had been eaten up for her old Christmas dinners, and if she would just stop the Christmases, they would see about gratitude. Wasn't it dreadful? And the very next day the little girl began to send letters to the Christmas Fairy, then telegrams, to stop it. But it didn't do any good; and then she got to calling at the Fairy's house, but the girl that came to the door always said, "Not at home," or "Engaged," or "At dinner," or something like that; and so it went on until it came to the old once-a-year Christmas Eve. The little girl fell asleep, and when she woke up in the morning—

"She found out it was all nothing but a dream," suggested the little girl.

"No, indeed!" said her papa. "It was all every bit true!"

"Well, what did she find out?"

"Why, that it wasn't Christmas at last, and wasn't ever going to be again. Now it's time for breakfast."

The little girl held her papa fast around the neck.

"You can't go if you're going to leave it so!"

"How do you want it left?"

"Christmas once a year."

"All right," said her papa, and he went on again.

The little girl went to thank the old Fairy because she had stopped its being Christmas, and she said she hoped she would keep her promise, and see that Christmas never, never came again. Then the Fairy frowned, and asked her if she was sure she knew what she meant; and the little girl asked her, why not? And the old Fairy said that now she was behaving just as greedily as ever, and she'd better look out. This made the little girl think it over carefully again, and she said she would be willing to have it Christmas about once in a thousand years; and then she said a hundred, and then she said ten, and at last she got down to one. Then the Fairy said that was the good old way that had pleased people ever since Christmas began, and she was agreed.

"How will that do?" asked the papa.

"First-rate!" said the little girl; but she hated to have the story stop, and was rather sober. However, Mamma put her head in at the door, and asked Papa:

"Are you coming to breakfast? What have you been telling that child?"

"Oh, just a moral tale."

The little girl caught him around the neck again.

"We know! Don't you tell what, Papa! Don't you tell what!"

Fads

The first newspaper "funnies" appeared in October of 1896 in the New York *Journal*. They were an immediate success with children, who finally found something for themselves in the family paper in the stories of "Happy Hooligan" and "The Captain and the Kids."

Mah-Jong invaded America in 1922. By the next year, Mah-Jong sets were selling better than radios. The craze for the incredibly complicated game was satirized by Eddie Cantor, who sang: "If you want to play the game, I'll tell you what to do, Buy a silk kimona and begin to raise a queue; get yourself a book of rules and study till it's clear, And you'll know the game when you've got whiskers down to here."

During the twenties, Richard Simon and Lincoln Schuster bought out their first book: a collection of crossword puzzles. Sales of the book were phenomenal and a crossword puzzle craze ensued. At the height of the fad, the Baltimore and Ohio Railroad placed dictionaries on trains for the convenience of puzzlers, and college teams competed against each other in tournaments. The University of Kentucky even offered a course on crossword puzzles.

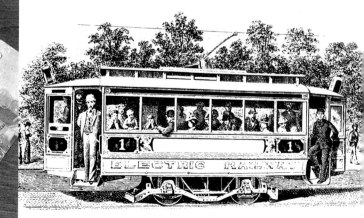

many ways, the automobile was the greatest
[fa]d of the 1910s and 1920s. This four-wheeled
[ve]hicle was the continuation of a series of
[w]heeled-fads in America, beginning with roller
[sk]ating, which swept the nation for a brief
[p]eriod in the 1870s, and bicycling, which
[ca]ught on in the 1890s.

Beginning in 1906, there was a new
favorite American family pastime:
reading the book series put out by the
Stratemeyer Literary Syndicate, which
included such timeless favorites as
The Bobbsey Twins, *The Hardy Boys*,
and *The Nancy Drew Mysteries*.

[Cr]oquet was a popular family pastime in
[th]e early years of the century. Some
[fa]natics couldn't get enough by daylight,
[a]nd purchased mallets with candle hold-
[er]s for night play.

[M]ONOPOLY was the family fad
[o]f the mid-thirties. In 1935, game
[se]ts sold at the rate of 20 million
[p]er week as depression-rocked
[fa]milies stayed at home and made
[th]eir fortunes on a game board.

[J]ust before the turn of the
[c]entury, bicycling was the
[gr]eat American fad. Weekend
[a]fternoons were devoted to
[r]ides around town and stage
[s]tars posed with their bicy-
[c]les for advertisements. The
[a]dvent of trolleys in 1900 put
[a] quick end to the fad.

Breakfast cereals were one fad of the
early twentieth century that stuck.
Whereas they had grown up on break-
fasts of bacon and eggs, fried potatoes,
sausage, and doughnuts, parents in the
1910s and 1920s began serving their
own children the new boxed breakfast
cereals made popular by businessmen
like J. H. Kellogg and C. W. Post, who
capitalized on the nation's new concern
with healthy eating and made their own
names household words.

FAMILY FEASTS

Richey the flower boy.

All together on the 4th.

A time to rest after dinner.
Uncle Joe & Sonny.

September 1913

The best cook

A ride through the park.

Picnic in the park with Danny tending the fire.

Sunday Dinner

Sundays used to mean two things to families: long hours at church in the morning and a special dinner in the afternoon. Sundays were a time for family; for our best clothes and for children's best grown-up manners. After long hours in church in the morning, children would do their best to stay quiet and clean while Mother went to the kitchen to prepare the feast. Sometimes the children would even be convinced to help prepare the meal! It was not necessarily an extravagant meal; but whatever the family finances allowed, parents always made sure that each Sunday dinner was a special time, a time to pause away from the distractions of the rest of the world and a time to be thankful for the comforting world of the family.

Menu for Sunday Dinner

Onion and Potato Soup

Roast Beef

Mashed Potatoes

Green Peas

Chocolate Cream Pie

Onion and Potato Soup

Take six potatoes, one onion, butter, three pints of water, one large tablespoonful of chopped parsley, the yolks of two eggs, pepper, and salt. Fry the potatoes and onion in the butter. When slightly colored put them into the boiling water and add parsley. Let it boil until the potatoes are quite soft and then press all through a colander. Return the puree to the fire and let it simmer for two or three minutes. When ready to serve have the well-beaten yolks ready and add a little of the soup to them, stirring all the time. When mixed, add them slowly to the soup, with plenty of salt and pepper. Do not let soup boil after adding the eggs.

Roast Beef

The cook must have her roaster clean and bright; a clear, brisk fire. It is impossible to give a specific rule as for time, but slow roasting is important. The season of the year—the length of time which the meat has been kept—all has an influence. As a general rule, a quarter of an hour to the pound is the best. The young and tender should be roasted; the strong and full-grown animal boiled or stewed. Basting is a most important operation in roasting, as the more meat is basted, the sooner and better it is roasted. Never pour gravy over either roasted or boiled joints, as many prefer the juices of the meats to gravy which is made.

A well-selected roasting piece of beef—the noble sirloin of about fifteen pounds—will require about three hours and a half. The beef should be kept for several days after it is killed, if the weather will allow; in winter a week.

Have ready the spit and roaster before putting it down. Rub the beef all over with white ground ginger—nothing else; never salt roasted meat, it draws out the juice; do not place it too near at first, but allow it to gradually warm; baste it well at first with a little cold water. When it begins to cook, pin a thick piece of paper on it to preserve the fat. Keep the fire clear and brisk. Continue every quarter of an hour to baste it. The last half hour remove the paper; then sprinkle over it a little salt, baste it with a little melted butter and dredge it with flour; then let it remain until the froth rises; then serve on a hot dish. Take the drippings, skim off all the fat, thicken the gravy with a very little browned flour, which is done by sifting the flour onto a tin plate and browning it in an oven. This is nice for all kinds of brown gravies.

A Practical Housekeeper, Cookery As It Should Be, 1856

FAMILY FEASTS

Mashed Potatoes

Boil 8 medium-sized potatoes until soft. Drain and dry out the soft potatoes by shaking the pan over heat. Put through a ricer and add three quarters of a tablespoon of salt. Heat one half cup of milk to just under boiling and melt in it 2 ounces of butter. Add the potatoes to the milk and butter mixture and beat well until light and fluffy.

Green Peas

First boil the pods, which are sweet and full of flavor, in a little water; skim them out, and add the peas, which boil until tender; add then a little butter, cream, pepper, and salt. If they are served as a garnish, do not add the juice; but if served alone, the juice is a savory addition. Time to cook, about half an hour.

Practical Cooking and Dinner Giving, 1878

Chocolate Cream Pie

Beat to a cream one-half cupful of butter and one and a quarter cupfuls of powdered sugar. Add two well-beaten eggs, a generous half-cupful of milk, and one and a half cupfuls of sifted flour, with which has been mixed one and one-half teaspoonfuls of baking powder. Bake this in four well-buttered, deep tin plates for about fifteen minutes in a moderate oven. Put one-half pint of milk in the double boiler and on the fire. Beat together the yolks of two eggs, three tablespoons of powdered sugar, and a level tablespoon of flour; stir this mixture into the boiling milk, beating well; add one-sixth teaspoonful of salt and cook for fifteen minutes, stirring often. When cooked, flavor with one-half teaspoonful of vanilla extract. Put two of the cakes on two large plates, spread the cream over them and lay the other two cakes on top. Beat the whites of two eggs to a stiff froth and then beat into them one cupful of powdered sugar and one teaspoonful of vanilla. Shave one ounce of chocolate and put it in a small pan with two tablespoonfuls of sugar and one tablespoonful of boiling water. Stir over a hot fire until smooth and glossy. Now add three tablespoonfuls of cream or milk and stir into the beaten egg and sugar. Spread on the pies and set away for a few hours.

Summer Breakfast

Breakfast was often the most casual meal of the day, but in most families it was still a time to come together before beginning the day. In summertime, breakfast was full of wonderful fresh fruits, whatever was in season. And it was an early meal, served before the heat of the day with the cool of the previous evening still lingering in the kitchen. A hearty summertime breakfast prepared the family for the day ahead.

Menu for Breakfast in June

Homegrown Strawberries

Omelets with Fresh Tomatoes

Johnny Cakes

Hash Brown Potatoes

Omelets with Fresh Tomatoes

Before beginning, boil three or four whole tomatoes for 2-3 minutes; set the tomatoes aside. Beat 2 eggs, add 2 tablespoons of milk and a pinch of salt and pepper. Heat 1 tablespoon of butter in an omelet pan until sizzling hot; pour in egg mixture. Cover the pan and cook the eggs for 1 full minute over medium heat. After the minute is up, take off the cover and gently lift the edges of the omelet. Tip the pan slightly to let the liquid egg from the top of the omelet run underneath. Cover again and cook about 2 minutes more until solid but still soft. The omelet should be browned on the bottom. Before folding the omelet in half, place the tomatoes in the center of the circle. Then fold one side of the omelet over the other enveloping the tomatoes. Serve omelet with tomato sauce poured around.

Hash Brown Potatoes

Chop 3 cups of raw potatoes into cubes. Grate 1 tablespoon of onion and chop 1 tablespoon parsley. Mix these three ingredients in a bowl with salt and black pepper. Heat 3 tablespoons of bacon drippings in a large skillet. Spread the potato mixture over the fat. Press the mixture with a broad knife or a plate into a cake. Saute the cake slowly, shaking the skillet from time to time to keep the potatoes from sticking. When the bottom is brown, cut the potato cake in half and turn each half with 2 spatulas.

Pour a quarter cup of cream over the two cakes. Continue cooking until second sides are brown. Serve straight from the skillet.

Afternoon Tea

The tradition of afternoon tea came to us originally from England. In the days when dinner was served at midday and was the main meal of the day, afternoon tea was the light evening meal. Many families held onto the custom of afternoon tea even after dinner had become an evening meal. Tea became a social time, a time for visiting with friends and neighbors, or simply for sitting down with family for a break from the day's activities.

Menu for an Afternoon Family Tea

Tea

Hot Chocolate

Sally Lunn Bread

Tea

The most approved method for black tea is to pour a small quantity of boiling water on the tea; let it stand on a hot stove (not to boil) for twenty minutes, then put it into the tea-pot intended for the table, and fill it with boiling water. In pouring out black tea into the cup always put in the sugar first, then the cream, and the tea last. It alters the flavor entirely to add the sugar or cream afterwards.

Every-Day Cookery for Every Family, 1868

Hot Chocolate

A nice preparation of chocolate is to grate half a cake of the best chocolate, and pour over it a pint of boiling water to dissolve the chocolate; then add a pint of fresh milk; let this all boil for five minutes, then beat up the yolk of two eggs very smoothly, and stir in; sweeten to the taste, and serve hot.

Every-Day Cookery for Every Family, 1868

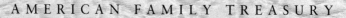

Sally Lunn Bread

Scald 1 cup of milk. Add a quarter cup of sugar, 2 teaspoons of salt, and 1 stick of butter. Let the mixture cool until it is lukewarm. Measure one half cup of very warm water into a large bowl. Sprinkle into the water one cake of dry or compressed yeast. Stir to dissolve yeast and add lukewarm milk mixture to yeast and water. Add 3 beaten eggs and 5 cups of sifted flour; beat until mixture is smooth.

Cover the dough and let rise in a warm place free from drafts. Let it rise until it is doubled in size, about 1 hour. Stir the mixture down and pour into 2 greased 8-inch square cake pans. Cover and let rise again, in a warm place free from drafts. Leave it about 30 minutes, until doubled.

Sprinkle the 2 breads with sugar, about 2 tablespoons each, and bake in a hot oven for about 25 minutes.

FAMILY FEASTS

Saturday Night Supper

On Saturday, the main family meal was supper, served about six o'clock in the evening. Saturdays were busy times, with shopping done in the morning and plenty of chores to fill the afternoon. And Saturday nights got busy, too, with concerts, walks downtown, or the weekly task of getting the children in the bathtub before church the next morning. But no matter what went on before or after, Saturday night supper was a time to come together and enjoy a simple, hearty meal in the comfort of the family home.

Menu for Saturday Night Supper

Chicken Pot Pie

Boston Baked Beans

New England Brown Bread

Bread Pudding

Chicken Pot Pie

Take a fat hen, dress it and cut it into pieces. Stew until tender, adding salt. Make a crust of two cups of sour cream, one-half teaspoonful of soda, a pinch of salt, one cup of butter, and one tablespoon of baking powder. Add enough flour to make a stiff dough.

Put the chicken into a deep pan with plenty of broth. Sprinkle in a handful of flour and add pepper and more salt if necessary. Wet the edge of pan and cover top with dough, about three-quarters of an inch thick, cutting a slit in the center for steam to escape. Bake the pie in a moderately hot oven for thirty minutes.

Boston Baked Beans

Take two quarts of middling sized white beans, three pounds of salt pork, and one spoonful of molasses. Pick the beans over carefully, wash and turn about a gallon of soft water to them in a pot; let them soak in it lukewarm overnight; set them in the morning where they will boil until the skin is very tender and about to break, adding a teaspoon of saleratus. Take them up dry, put them in your dish, stir in the molasses, gash the pork, and put down in the dish so as to have the beans cover all but the upper surface; turn in cold water until the top is just covered; bake and let the beans remain in the oven all night.

The Improved Housewife, 1870

New England Brown Bread

Take equal portions of sifted rye and Indian meal, mix them well together; add half a teaspoon of molasses, and two gills of good yeast, to about three quarts of the mixed meal. Wet this with good new milk, sufficient to make a dough that can be easily worked, even with one hand. For economy's sake, milk that has stood for twelve hours, and from which the cream has been taken, may be a substitute for new milk; or water which has been pressed from boiled squash, or in which squash has been boiled, is a much better substitute than pure water. But warm water is more commonly used. The ingredients should be thoroughly mixed, and stand, in cold weather, for twelve hours; in warm weather, two hours may be sufficient before baking. If baked in a brick oven, a three quart loaf should stand in the oven all night. The same quantity in three baking pans will bake in about three hours. Serve this warm from the oven, with good, sweet butter.

The American Practical Cookery Book, 1861

Bread Pudding

Trim the crusts off six slices of stale bread. Cut the slices into cubes. Place all of the bread cubes into a buttered pudding dish. Mix together one quart of milk, one-half cup of sugar, one-half teaspoon of salt, three slightly beaten eggs, and a quarter teaspoon of cinnamon. Pour this mixture into the pudding dish on top of bread cubes. Cut two tablespoons of butter into small pieces and spread on top of the mixture in pudding dish. Bake for about an hour in a slow oven. Serve warm or cold with thick cream.

FAMILY FEASTS

Family Recreation

Baseball became America's favorite spectator sport in 1915. *Harper's* Magazine reported that "the fascination of the game has seized upon the American people, irrespective of age, sex, or other condition." Professional baseball was the first such public event to make the playing of "The Star Spangled Banner" a necessary opening event.

Saturday afternoon at the movies was often the one family entertainment outside the home in the 1920s and 1930s. Usually a double feature, the event was well worth the 5 or 10 cent admission.

A favorite family recreation at the turn of the century was the picnic. The picnic season began with Decoration Day in May and ended with Labor Day. In between, as one British tourist noted, "picnics are going off in every direction—quiet little church picnics, Sunday school picnics, working people's picnics . . . picnics of a hundred societies and associations." The highlight of the summer picnic season was the Fourth of July.

A trip to the amusement park was a must for most working families at least a couple of times each year in the 1910s and 1920s. Every major city had a nearby park—Revere Beach in Boston, Willow Grove in Philadelphia, The Chutes in San Francisco, and the greatest of them all, Coney Island in Brooklyn. Rides like the roller coaster and the ferris wheel offered thrills for all ages at a cost of 5 or 10 cents a ride.

efore moving indoors in 1956, Ringling ros. and Barnum & Bailey Circus per- rmed under a 10,000 seat tent. Modern renas have replaced the giant tent city at traveled with the Show and which equired 1,000 workingmen to set up and reak down each day.

In the early part of the twentieth century, Chautauqua provided entertainment and education for rural American families. The Chautauqua circuit brought big-city shows and speakers to isolated small towns and gave residents the chance for a special day out together.

Use courtesy of Ringling Bros.-Barnum & Bailey Combined Shows, Inc.

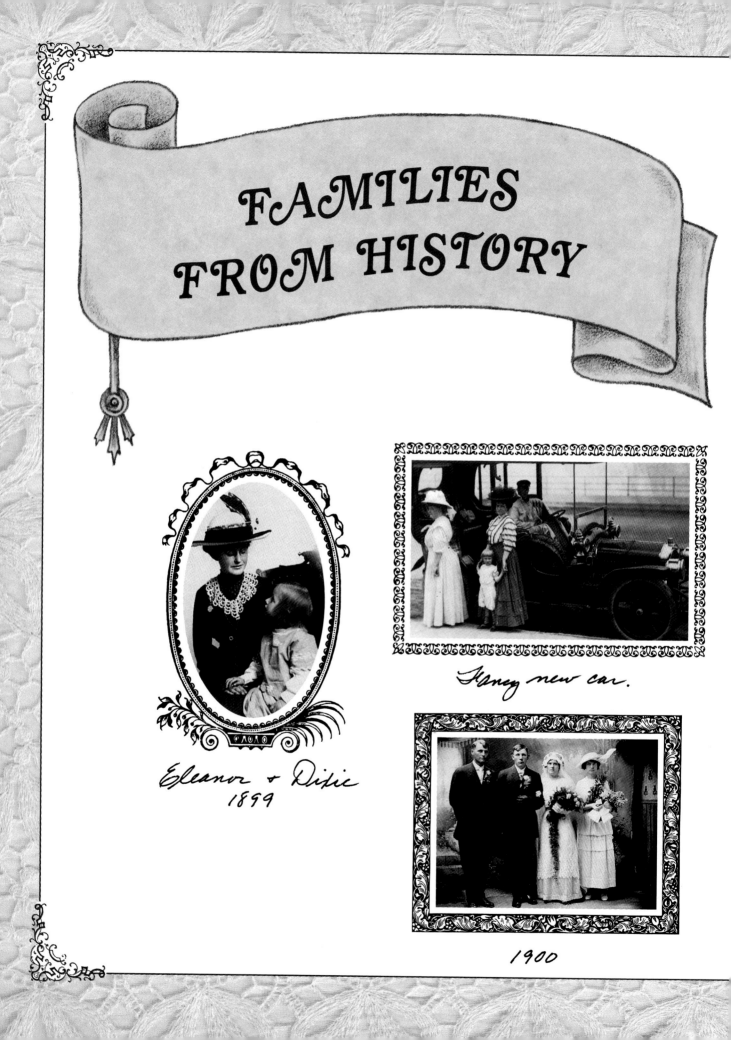

FAMILIES FROM HISTORY

Eleanor & Dixie
1899

Fancy new car.

1900

Ted + Teddy Jr.

*By the shade of the old oak.
1901*

*Ready for the
train trip.*

All together now. 1901

His Good Stepmother

from *Abraham Lincoln* by Genevieve Foster

A whole year passed in misery and loneliness. Then Abe's father couldn't stand it any longer. He went back to Kentucky, leaving Abe and Sarah alone with Dennis Hanks. Dennis had come to live in their cabin after Aunt Betsey died.

One dismal December day, Abe sat by the fire scratching all the letters he could remember in the ashes, wishing he knew how to read. Every day seemed like a week, waiting for his father to come back. Abe knew why he'd gone, but that didn't make waiting any easier. Dennis had just come in with his gun, bringing a squirrel for dinner. Sarah said she'd cook it and try to make it taste good. Abe said he couldn't eat. He couldn't even swallow.

What if nobody would come? he thought. Or what if somebody came, and she didn't like them—him and Sarah? What if... all of a sudden he heard horses' hooves. He ran outside. And almost before he knew it, SHE was there. His stepmother, Sarah Bush Lincoln. He saw her first, sitting beside his father on the seat of a big wagon, piled so high with furniture that it took four horses to pull it.

On top of the pile sat two girls and a boy. They jumped down as the wagon stopped and stood staring at Abe and Sarah in their dirty, ragged clothes. Then the tall, straight woman came and stood beside them,

"These are my children," she said. "John and Sarah and Matilda Johnston." Her voice was warm and friendly. "And I suppose you are Sarah Lincoln? And you," she added slowly, "you must be Abraham."

Abe looked up. Her eyes were as friendly as her voice. She didn't even seem to see that he was too tall, or mind that he was homely. She just smiled, and so Abe smiled, too.

From then to the end of his life, this second mother was to be "the best friend he had."

"Wa-al now," she said briskly, stepping into the cabin. "Fust thing for me to do is to make something for us all to eat. Meantime, you young-uns go out to the horse trough. Take this soft soap and wash up good, all over."

Wash up? thought Abe, all over? in the winter? That was a mighty queer notion. But he did it, and it felt good. It felt good, too, to have a comb run through his gritty black hair. And to put on a clean shirt of the Johnston boy's. And to sit down to good, hot food with eight folks around the table to eat it.

Next morning, his new mother swept up the dirty cabin. But to be halfway decent, she told Abe's father, it would have to have a wood floor and a door and windows. Then he could get some lime over to Gentryville and whitewash the walls. Right away, that night, everybody must help carry in the furniture and unroll the feather beds. Abe heard something bumping in the chest as they set it down.

Next morning, his stepmother opened it; there were two books. One was the Bible. And the other—he could hardly believe his eyes—the other was his beloved fable book.

It was *Aesop's Fables.*

"Kin you read?" his stepmother asked. Abe shook his head. "Nor kin I," she added quickly. "But you'd like to learn?" She knew the answer before he gave it. "Then I'll make sure you get the chance, soon as there's enough settlers around here to have a school start up."

The winter Abe was thirteen, a school was started. All the children went for a few months. The others didn't half try, but Abe was different. He went over and over the

AMERICAN FAMILY TREASURY

words in the Speller, and practiced writing everywhere, especially on the back of the big wooden fire shovel.

Dennis got interested, and made a pen for him out of a turkey buzzard's quill, stirred up some ink, and brought back some paper from the store at Gentryville to make a notebook. In it Abe wrote:

Abraham Lincoln,
his hand and pen
He will be good,
but God knows when.

He was now fourteen. At last he could read and write. All day long, his father had chores for him to do—hard, grubby work—but as soon as he could lay down his axe and hoe, he was turning the pages of a book, reading as if he were starved.

Tom Lincoln couldn't understand it. "It'd be different," he'd say, "if he was puny or sickly, so's he couldn't go huntin'. But for a big strappin' feller like Abe to take so to book-larnin' is jes' plain queer."

But the good stepmother understood this boy who was so different from the others. Sometimes, as she was patching or knitting he'd have her listen while he read a funny story aloud, and they'd laugh over it together.

The first book Abe ever owned, he got from the first man he ever worked for, Mr. Josiah Crawford, a nearby farmer.

Mr. Crawford was a thin, sour man, with such a way of hanging onto money that he had more of it than any of his neighbors,

and could hire them to work for him. . . .

Josiah didn't care much about books, but he owned a few. He let Abe take one home, warning him to be careful with it. It was a biography of George Washington.

Abe could hardly wait to start it, and then he couldn't bear to stop. He read all evening, stretched out by the fire, until his father banked it with ashes and made him go to bed. Abe slept in the loft. To have the book handy as soon as it grew light, he carried it up with him and laid it carefully between the logs. Next morning when he reached for it, his heart sank. It was soaking wet. There had been rain in the night. What could he do or say?

"Wa-al," said Josiah Crawford, shrewdly. "Seein' it's you, Abe . . . You put in three days huskin' corn, and you kin keep it."

Only three days! Abe could hardly believe it. When those three days were over the book belonged to him. The story of George Washington's life. He read it again and again. Each time it stirred him with ambition.

"I'm not always going to grub and shuck corn and split rails for a livin'," he said to Mrs. Crawford one morning. And when she asked him what he wanted to do or be, he answered, "The President." He half smiled as if he were joking, but his voice was serious. "Well, anyway, I'll study and get ready," he said, "and the chance may come."

FAMILIES FROM HISTORY

The Lincoln Pets

from *The White House* Pets by Margaret Truman

One of the few pets Abraham Lincoln had during his childhood was a pig. Those who work with pigs maintain that they are extremely intelligent. Lincoln's boyhood pig must have been one of the smartest ever, for the youngster taught it to play hide-and-seek. When the pig grew to full size, it turned out to be a big one, and Abe rode on its back as though it were a pony.

Perhaps because he remembered this pet so well, years later Mr. Lincoln played the role of a rescuer to a pig. One of the tales told most often about him has to do with a pig that was stuck in the mud at the side of the road. Young lawyer Lincoln was riding by, saw the pig's plight, waded into the mud, and freed the screaming animal, setting it on firmer ground. The pig departed without a backward glance, leaving a mud-spattered Lincoln to endure the jibes of his traveling companions.

Aside from the horse he needed for transportation, there is no record of any special Lincoln pets during his bachelor days nor immediately after he married Mary Todd. It was said that she did not want any animals in her house. . . .

In Springfield, the family usually kept cats, and Mrs. Lincoln referred to them as her husband's "hobby." He would often sit down on the floor and talk to one or another of them and play gently with them.

Another pet was a medium-sized, yellow-brown mongrel pup named Fido. To be accurate, only half of Fido belonged to Willy and Tad Lincoln. The other half belonged to the Roll family who lived down the block. The Lincoln and Roll boys were long-time friends, and they reached an agreement whereby they shared the dog. Fido heartily approved of this arrangement because by moving back and forth between the two houses he sometimes managed to get two dinners. The pup must have had a winning personality, because Mrs. Lincoln allowed him to curl up on the boys' beds.

Abraham Lincoln often enjoyed a frolic on the floor with the boys and Fido, and Lincoln buffs insist that it was Fido who inspired one of his favorite parables. While rolling on the floor during an evening romp with the dog and his sons, Mr. Lincoln suddenly asked,

"If you were to call a tail a leg, how many legs would this dog have?" Five was the answer the boys gave.

"No," replied Lincoln, "calling a tail a leg does not make it a leg."

Why Fido did not accompany the Lincolns to the White House has never been fully explained. One version has it that the railroad did not allow dogs aboard trains in those days. But surely this rule would have been suspended for a President-elect. It is also possible that Mr. Lincoln believed that a half-ownership did not entitle Willy and Tad to take the dog permanently. For whatever reason, Fido was left behind to get along as best he could with one set of masters. . . .

Tad and Willy were promised a couple of ponies when they were settled in at the White House, and the President was as good as his word. Soon Tad and Willy—they were inseparable—were clopping through the streets of Washington with Mr. Lincoln astride his own horse tailing not too far behind.

In addition to the ponies, Tad was presented with a dog and Willy was given a cat. These two animals created quite a stir among the White House staff, for on the same day

AMERICAN FAMILY TREASURY

the dog had pups and the cat had kittens. News of the multiple births was circulated through Congress, the Cabinet, and the foreign legations. The one who leaked the information, and boasted about it, too—was Abraham Lincoln himself. He even had a hand in thinking up new names for the pups and kittens in both litters.

The death of little Willy only a year after he came to Washington was a crushing blow to the Lincolns. Tad especially felt the loss. He became listless, hollow-eyed; his pony remained in the stables, unridden and unpetted. As he explained his feelings, "The ponies make me miss Willy even more." Later Lincoln himself was deeply saddened when Willy's and Tad's ponies died in a stable fire in the winter of 1864. The President had rushed out in the night and tried unsuccessfully to rescue them, but it was too late.

The sight of Tad moping around the Executive mansion was almost more than President Lincoln could bear. Before the tragedy, he had been a high-spirited, first-class mischief-maker. That was how he received his nickname. Tad had been christened Thomas, but he was such a fidgeter, so "wriggly," that Mr. Lincoln dubbed him Tadpole, later shortening it to Tad.

The President tried to restore his son to his usually mischievous self by giving him other pets, and people also sent Tad pets. From Philadelphia came a pair of pink-eyed white rabbits. . . . .

Tad often stroked their soft, silky fur, but nothing aroused that gleam that shines in the eyes of a small boy when he receives a pet he really likes. Happily, that was solved by a pair of goats.

Modern city dwellers accustomed to dogs and cats, birds, and other small animals may not realize how popular goats were as pets a hundred years ago. They eat practically anything they can get close to, the female gives milk, and children can hitch them to small carts.

Mr. and Mrs. Lincoln and Tad went riding one day, and Tad saw some goats. For the first time in months the boy began to smile as he watched them chew up a few things.

Noting his son's interest, the President instructed an aide, Mr. William Tisdale, to scout around and come back with a pair of goats. Mr. Tisdale found a pretty good pair that he bought at five dollars each.

The President commented on the trouble they might cause Mr. Tisdale, and when the aide asked how, Mr. Lincoln said that Tad wouldn't give him any peace until there was a harness for the goats. Tisdale was only too glad to get the saddler of the nearby cavalry company to make the proper gear.

The goats were immediately named Nanny and Nanko, and for the next few months, the White House was a happy bedlam of noise.

Tad had never owned a goat before, and with the typical inquisitive approach of a ten-year-old, he tried to find out just how much fun he could have with them. He tied a rope to their collars and pretended they were oversize dogs. That was a rather tame sport. Tad tried butting them in the head, but they butted back, so there was no use in pursuing that.

He turned the goats loose and chased after them, whooping and yelling as he raced across the lawn. That wasn't such a good idea, for the goats got into the flower beds, causing Mr. Watt, the White House gardener, to turn purple with rage as he saw a prize iris being trampled under their hoofs. Mr. Watt, knowing how these animals chewed shrubs and flowers, never was a goat admirer anyway.

In time, the goats were broken to the harness and learned to pull a cart. Then Tad, with the children of the aides and neighbors, would pile into the wagon and go shrieking around the grounds, barreling through flower beds, shrubs, and over freshly sown

FAMILIES FROM HISTORY

ground. It is said that Mr. Watt was heard to mutter dark threats against Tad's goats.

On one occasion, the goats ran afoul of Mrs. Lincoln when they appeared inside the White House, and she never did quite forgive them. The first time she knew of it was when they showed up in the kitchen looking for a handout. . . .

AMERICAN FAMILY TREASURY

The team of Nanny and Nanko was disbanded while Tad was accompanying his mother on a trip to Vermont. The boy had exacted a promise that his father would see to it the goats were cared for and would issue periodic reports on their welfare. The President received a letter from Mary asking that money be sent to her and ending: "Tad says are the goats well?"

Lincoln answered sending the money and concluding: "Tell Tad the goats and father are very well—especially the goats."

Mr. Lincoln tried his best to look after the goats and the Civil War at the same time, but the two tasks were more than any president could handle. That was more the goats' fault than his.

Nanko was the better behaved of the pair, although both were frisky, but at least Nanko stayed put in the stables, while Nanny kept getting out and making a beeline for the flowers.

Finally, to keep Mr. Watt from having apoplexy, the President had Nanny brought into the White House. Nanny wandered forlornly through the corridors, got on Tad's bed and curled up, contentedly chewing her cud. Mrs. Cuthbert, the housekeeper, promptly chased her out of the room.

For a couple of days, Nanny ambled aimlessly around and then finally managed to get back outside, whereupon she made for the flowers again. This time Mr. Watts saw her first.

And so President Lincoln sat down to compose a letter to his wife. The first two sentences concerned family financial matters, and then the letter continued:

"I suppose you are glad to learn this. Tell dear Tad, poor Nanny goat is lost, and Mrs. Cuthbert and I are in distress about it. The day you left, Nanny was found resting herself and chewing her cud in the middle of Tad's bed. But now she's gone! The gardener kept complaining that she destroyed the flowers till it was concluded to bring her down to the White House. This was done and the second day she had disappeared, and has not been heard of since. This is the last we know of poor Nanny."

The departure of Nanny by no means brought an end to Tad Lincoln's string of pets. There was always Nanko. And Tad found other interests. He expressed a desire to raise pigeons; nobody objected to this except the White House caretakers. The birds multiplied rapidly and did the kind of damage pigeons had long been noted for.

Then there was the matter of a turkey named Jack, which a family friend sent to the White House to serve as the First Family's 1863 Christmas dinner. Tad wasn't aware of the bird's ultimate fate—to him Jack was one more pet to have fun with. Tad and the turkey became great pals, with Jack following the boy everywhere he went.

But shortly before Christmas, Tad found out the dinner menu and ran sobbing and wailing to his father. The president was in the midst of an important meeting, but he always had time for Tad. He listened carefully to his son's tearful plea, then hastily wrote some words on a card. It was a reprieve for the turkey, who soon became a White House fixture.

The turkey came to the President's attention again later under much more pleasant circumstances. During the 1864 election, soldiers stationed in Washington were permitted absentee votes at a special facility set up on the White House grounds. The President, Tad, and Noah Brooks, a noted newspaper reporter for the Sacramento *Daily Union* . . . were at the window peering through the rain at a line of soldiers waiting to cast their ballots. Suddenly Jack strutted in among them.

"Why is your turkey at the polls?" the President asked his son, "Does he vote?"

"No," replied Tad, flashing a bit of his father's famous wit, "he is not of age yet."

It was a story Mr. Lincoln repeated with a grin to many of his associates.

FAMILIES FROM HISTORY

The Boys of My Boyhood

William Cullen Bryant

The boys of the generation to which I belonged—that is to say, who were born in the last years of the last century or the earliest of this—were brought up under a system of discipline which put a far greater distance between parents and their children than now exists. The parents seemed to think this necessary in order to secure obedience. They were believers in the old maxim that familiarity breeds contempt. My own parents lived in the house with my grandfather and grandmother on the mother's side. My grandfather was a disciplinarian of the stricter sort, and I can hardly find words to express the awe in which I stood of him—an awe so great as almost to prevent anything like affection on my part, although he was in the main kind, and, certainly, never thought of being severe beyond what was necessary to maintain a certain degree of order in the family.

The other boys in that part of the country, my schoolmates and playfellows, were educated on the same system. Yet there were at the same time indications that this very severe discipline was beginning to relax. With my father and mother I was on much easier terms than with my grandfather. If a favor was to be asked of my grandfather, it was asked with fear and trembling; the request was postponed to the last moment, and then made with hesitation and blushes and a confused utterance.

One of the means of keeping the boys of that generation in order was a little bundle of birchen rods, bound together by a small cord, and generally suspended on a nail against the kitchen wall. This was esteemed as much a part of the necessary furniture as the crane that hung in the kitchen fireplace, or the shovel and tongs. It sometimes happened that the boy suffered a fate similar to that of the eagle in the fable, wounded by an arrow fledged with a feather from his own wing; in other words, the boy was made to gather the twigs intended for his own castigation.

The awe in which the boys of that time held their parents extended to all elderly persons, toward whom our behavior was more than merely respectful, for we all observed a hushed and subdued demeanor in their presence. Toward the ministers of the gospel this behavior was particularly marked. At that time, every township in Massachusetts had its minister, who was settled there for life, and when he once came among his people was understood to have entered into a connection with them scarcely less lasting than the marriage tie.

The community in which he lived regarded him with great veneration, and the visits which from time to time he made to the district schools seemed to the boys important occasions, for which special preparation was made. When he came to visit the school which I attended, we all had on our Sunday clothes, and we were ready for him with a few answers to the questions in the Westminster Catechism. He heard us recite our lessons, examined us in the catechism, and then began a little address, which I remember was the same on every occasion. He told us how much greater were the advantages of education which we enjoyed than those which had fallen to the lot of our parents, and exhorted us to make the best possible use of them, both for our own sakes and that of our parents, who were ready to make any sacrifice for us, even so far as to take the bread out of their own mouth to give us. I can remember being disgusted with this illustration of parental kindness which I was obliged to listen to twice at least in every year.

AMERICAN FAMILY TREASURY

TR: Children's Hero

from *Theodore Roosevelt: The Man as I Knew Him* by Nicholas Roosevelt

My earliest recollections of Theodore Roosevelt go back to summers at Oyster Bay, at the turn of the century, when sixteen children of Roosevelt cousins spent much of their time playing together. All but one of the sixteen were born between 1883 and 1894. I was among the three youngest. We liked nothing better than to have TR as leader in group games and outings. To be with him was to have fun, if for no other reason than that he was so obviously having a good time himself. As Lincoln Steffens aptly phrased it: "The gift of the gods to Theodore Roosevelt was joy—joy in life." He loved to play, but he also loved his work, and in both he applied literally the injunction in the Book of Ecclesiastes: "Whatsoever thy hand findeth to do, do it with thy might." We knew that TR scorned cowardice, meanness and evasiveness and that he expected obedience. But we also knew that he was scrupulously fair and that he would even intercede on our behalf when our mothers took a dim view of our conduct if he thought that we deserved it. This, of course, strengthened our feeling that even though he was one of the grownups he was at heart our friend and ally.

Just as children loved TR, so he loved children—his own, their cousins, his grand-

We liked nothing better than to have TR as leader in group games and outings. To be with him was to have fun, if for no other reason than that he was so obviously having a good time himself. As Lincoln Steffens aptly phrased it "The gift of the gods to Theodore Roosevelt was joy—joy in life.'

children, all children. The mothers often chided him (but gently!) for picking up a sleeping baby and cuddling it. As soon as a child learned to walk he would solemnly accompany it hand-in-hand on adventurous journeys about the nursery or in the garden, and as the children grew older he went through a regular romping ritual with each, including pillow fights and playing bear. Even those of us who were very young were struck by his irrepressible cheerfulness and by his genuine interest in each of his young relatives.

When TR joined in our games he did so with gusto, and I think that often he enjoyed them as much—or even more—than we did. His close friend, Owen Wister, was right in insisting that deep in him was what Shakespeare called "the boy eternal." In rainy weather our favorite game, in which he happily took part, was hide-and-seek in the Old Barn. This barn no longer stands. Its frame was made of heavy hand-hewn beams of white oak, almost a foot in width, that bound the sides of the barn together and held up the roof. The hay usually was piled somewhat higher than the first tier of the cross beams, with the result that under each beam was a tunnel through which small boys easily scrambled, to be followed (not so eas-

AMERICAN FAMILY TREASURY

ily) by the rather stout President of the United States cheerfully trying to force his way through passages that even some of the older children found tight. It was characteristic of TR's boyishness and sense of fun that he liked to try to induce a member of the cabinet or other visiting dignitary to join in these games—and such was his persuasiveness that a few succumbed despite the sticky heat of a wet Long Island summer day. The only cabinet member whom I clearly remember joining in these games was the Attorney General, William H. Moody, but I am sure that if TR could have induced the austere and wiry Secretary of State Elihu Root, or the somewhat pompous and paunchy Senator Chauncey M. Depew or Ambassador Joseph H. Choate to join us, he would have done so with glee.

Another of the best-loved group activities was cross-country hiking. TR was the leader, and it was part of the fun—and without our knowing it, the discipline—that each child followed the leader in single file. This meant that if TR climbed over large log or waded through a stream or muddy pond it was up to each youngster to do as he did, without evasion or complaint. We loved it, although the mothers disapproved, particularly when we came home soaked. It was after a chilling autumn hike that Mrs. Roosevelt decreed, on seeing her wet brood, that all had to be dosed with a bitter drug then thought to be a cold preventative. The tradi-

Just as children loved TR, so he loved children—his own, their cousins, his grandchildren, all children. The mothers often chided him (but gently!) for picking up a sleeping baby and cuddling it. As soon as a child learned to walk he would solemnly accompany it hand-in-hand on adventurous journeys about the nursery.

tion is that Kermit, perhaps ten or twelve years old, went to his father and ruefully said: "She says that I've got to take the stuff. Can't you do something to stop her?" To which TR is reputed to have replied: "Kermit, I'll be lucky if she doesn't make me take it also!" How the other Roosevelt parents felt about his soaking us on a hike may be judged from the fact that on one such occasion my mother, who could be a tart when mad, upbraided my sister, who had been on the hike, for getting wet. When my sister tried to exculpate herself by explaining that she was simply following her cousin Theodore, who was the leader, my mother said sharply: "Just because your cousin Theodore behaves like an idiot is no reason why you should behave like an idiot."

Unlike the other Roosevelts of his generation, TR never cared for sailing, but he loved to row. I suspect that the reason for this was that it was a good form of exercise for his vigorous frame and that it gave him a chance to be with his wife without other company. Many days each summer the two spent hours alone on Cold Spring Harbor, eating their lunch on the beach, happily free from the intrusion of curiosity seekers.

When we went on overnight camping trips, which were for boys only, Archie and I usually went with him as steersmen. The two of us would huddle in the stern, comfortable and happy at the prospect of the camping trip, while he, rowing vigorously, was

FAMILIES FROM HISTORY

equally happy—but far from comfortable because of the heat of Long Island's summer afternoons. Many is the hour that I spent as a small boy watching the sweat drip from his square forehead, nose, and straggly moustache as he pulled the short, quick strokes of a skilled oarsman. Sometimes he rowed in silence, but he was always glad to talk with us about what we had been doing or books we were reading or things that concerned him.

Our favorite overnight camping place was known as Fox Point, on the Sound side of Lloyd's Neck. At this spot there was plenty of driftwood for the campfire. Under his supervision we followed a fixed routine: drawing up the unloaded boats (the older boys had come by themselves) out of reach of the tide and carrying food and blankets to the campground; gathering wood; staking out each youngster's

The marvel is that with all the burdens of his official duties he not only made time to play with his children and their young cousins, but that he got so much fun out of his own relations with the youngsters.

sleeping spot; then, weather and tide (and TR) permitting, we stripped and swam in the Sound. The older boys then started the fire, and when it was well burned down, TR acted as chef, the fare usually consisting of chickens or steaks done in bacon fat. My own recollection is that he fried the meat in a good deal of fat, but Archie, who after fifty years of trial and error has become a good roaster, insists that his father, in fact, boiled the steak in grease. Whatever TR did with the food, we ate it greedily, sure that there was no better cook anywhere. Unless we had made a late start the favorite accompaniments were potatoes baked in coals and lots of bread and butter, usually with a generous mixture of sand.

With dusk came a main part of the ritual—his telling us ghost stories, of which he remembered many. Usually someone called for a particular oft-told tale, to which the older boys listened as carefully as the younger ones. Each of his four sons was quick to call TR's attention to any departure from his usual recital—a correction that he took with his ever-present good humor. I can see that these camping trip must have given him relief from the gruelling demands and restrictions of the presidency. Neither Archie nor I remember any secret service men or guards, even at a distance, when we camped on Lloyd's Neck. . . .

No wonder that as children we adored this warm-hearted companion. The marvel is that with all the burdens of his official duties he not only made time to play with his children and their young cousins, but that he got so much fun out of his own relations with the youngsters, including even taking telephone messages for them. His daughter, Ethel Derby, remembers hearing the telephone ring at Sagamore as they were going in to breakfast—this was while he was still president— and his picking up the receiver and then grinning with delight. When he hung up, he reported the following conversation:

Small Boy: "Is that you Archie?"

TR: "No. This is Archie's father."

Small Boy: "Oh, well, you'll do. Tell Archie to be sure to come to supper tonight. Now don't forget," and the small boy hung up. Whereupon TR quoted from Lewis Carroll: "How the creatures do order one about!"

AMERICAN FAMILY TREASURY

FAMILIES FROM HISTORY

On Being a Granddaughter

from Blackberry Winter by Margaret Mead

My paternal grandmother, who lived with us from the time my parents married until she died in 1927, while I was studying anthropological collections in German museums, was the most decisive influence on my life. She sat at the center of our household. Her room—and my mother always saw to it that she had the best room, spacious and sunny, with a fireplace if possible—was the place to which we immediately went when we came in from playing or home from school. There my father went when he arrived in the house. There we did our lessons on the cherry-wood table with which she had begun housekeeping and which, later, was my dining room table for twenty-five years. There, sitting by the fire, erect and intense, she listened to us and to all of Mother's friends and to our friends. In my early childhood she was also very active—cooking, preserving, growing flowers in the garden, and attentive to all the activities of the country and the farm, including the chickens that were always invading the lawn and that I was always being called from my book to shoo away.

My mother was trustworthy in all matters that concerned our care. Grandma was trustworthy in quite a different way. She meant exactly what she said, always. If you borrowed her scissors, you returned them. In like case, Mother would wail ineffectually, "Why does everybody borrow my scissors and never return them?" and Father would often utter idle threats. But Grandma never threatened. She never raised her voice. She simply commanded respect and obedience by her complete expectation that she would be obeyed. And she never gave silly orders. She became my model when, in later life, I tried to formulate a role for the modern parent who can no longer exact obedience merely by virtue of being a parent and yet must be able to get obedience when it is necessary. Grandma never said, "Do this because Grandma says so," or "because Grandma says you have to do it." She simply said, "Do it," and I knew from her tone of voice that it was necessary.

But Grandma never threatened. She never raised her voice. She simply commanded respect and obedience by her complete expectation that she would be obeyed. And she never gave silly orders. She became my model when, in later life, I tried to formulate a role for the modern parent who can no longer exact obedience merely by virtue of being a parent . . .

My grandmother grew up in the little town of Winchester, in Adams County, Ohio, which two of my great-great-grandfathers had founded. She was one of nine children who reached adulthood. Her father was a farmer, a small entrepreneur, a member of the state legislature, a justice of the peace, and the Methodist local preacher. . . . My

AMERICAN FAMILY TREASURY

grandmother began teaching school quite young, at a time when it was still somewhat unusual for a girl to teach school. When my grandfather, who was also a teacher, came home from the Civil War, he married my grandmother and they went to college together. They also graduated together. She gave the graduation address in the morning and my grandfather, who gave one in the afternoon, was introduced as the husband of Mrs. Mead who spoke in the morning. . . .

With the exception of the two years I went to kindergarten, for Grandma believed in training the hands early, though not with too fine work, and the year I was eight, when I went to school for a half-day in the fourth grade in Swarthmore, she taught me until I went to high school and even then helped me with my lessons when my teachers were woefully inadequate, as they often were. I never expected any teacher to know as much as my parents or grandmother did. Although my grandmother had no Greek, she had a good deal of Latin, and I remember that once, on the Fourth of July, she picked up one of my brother's Latin texts because she had never read Sallust.

She was conscious of the developmental differences between boys and girls and considered boys to be much more vulnerable and in need of patience from their teachers than were girls of the same age. This was part of the background of my learning the meaning of gender. And just as Grandma thought that boys were more vulnerable, my father thought it was easier for girls to do well in school, and so he always required me to get two and a half points higher than my brother in order to win the same financial bonus.

Because Grandma did so many things with her hands, a little girl could always tag after her, talking and asking questions and listening. Side by side with Grandma I learned to peel apples, to take the skin off tomatoes by plunging them into scalding water, to do simple embroidery stitches, and to knit. Later, during World War I, when I had to cook for the whole household, she taught me a lot about cooking, for example, just when to add a lump of butter, something that always had to be concealed from Mother, who thought that cooking with butter was extravagant. . . .

Mother never ceased to resent the fact that Grandma lived with us, but she gave her her due. Grandma never "interfered"—never tried to teach the children anything religious that had not been previously introduced by my mother, and in disagreements between my mother and father, she always took my mother's side. When my father threatened to leave my mother, my Grandma told him firmly that she would stay with her and the children.

When Grandma was angry, she sat and held her tongue. I used to believe that this involved some very mysterious internal, anatomical tick. She was so still, so angry, and so determined not to speak, not to lose her temper. And she never did. But not losing her temper came out of her eyes like fire. Years later, when I was given a picture of her as a young woman, I felt that I had looked very like her at the same age. But when I actually compared pictures of me with the one of her, I looked milky mild. Not until the birth of her great-great-granddaughter, my daughter's daughter Sevanne Margaret, did that flashing glance reappear in the family. Looking at her black eyes, inherited from her Armenian father, I see again shining out of them the flash of Martha Ramsey's furiousness.

I think it was Grandma who gave me my ease in being a woman. She was unquestionably feminine—small and dainty and pretty and wholly without masculine protest or feminine aggrievement. She had gone to college when this was a very unusual thing for a girl to do, she had a firm grasp of anything she paid attention to, she had married and

FAMILIES FROM HISTORY

had a child, and she had a career of her own. All this was true of my mother, as well. But my mother was filled with passionate resentment about the condition of women, as might my grandmother have been if my grandfather had lived and she had borne five children and had little opportunity to use her special gifts and training. As it was, the two women I knew best were mothers and had professional training. So I had no reason to doubt that brains were suitable for a woman. And as I had my father's kind of mind—which was also his mother's—I learned that the mind is not sex-typed.

Side by side with Grandma I learned to peel apples, to . . . do simple embroidery stitches, and to knit.

The content of my conscience came from my mother's concern for other people and the state of the world and from my father's insistence that the only thing worth doing is to add to the store of exactly known facts. But the strength of my conscience came from Grandma, who meant what she said. Perhaps nothing is more valuable for a child than living with an adult who is firm and loving—and Grandma was loving. I loved the feel of her soft skin, but she would never let me give her an extra kiss when I said good night.

After I left home I used to write long letters to Grandma, and later, when I went to Samoa, it was for Grandma that I tried to make clear what I was doing. She was not entirely happy with my choice of a career; she thought that botany would have been better than savages. Even though she herself hardly ever went to church—she had decided that she had gone to church enough—she taught me to treat all people as the children of God. But she had no way to include in her conception of human beings the unknown peoples of distant South Sea islands. When I was a child and would come into her room

with my hair flying, she would tell me I looked like the wild man of Borneo. For her, that was only a figure of speech.

Throughout my childhood she talked a great deal about teachers, about their problems and conflicts, and about those teachers who could never close the schoolhouse door behind them. The sense she gave me of what teachers are like, undistorted by my own particular experience with teachers, made me want to write my first book about adolescents in such a way that teachers of adolescents would understand it. Grandma always wanted to understand things, and she was willing to listen or read until she did. . . .

When I returned from Samoa, Grandma had already left for Fairhope, Alabama, where she had taken my two younger sisters to an experimental school. So I never had a chance to follow up the letters I wrote her from Samoa with long talks through which she would have understood more about what I was doing, and I would have learned more about how to say things useful to teachers.

In her later years, she devoted herself with almost single-minded passion to my sister Elizabeth, the one of us who was least like the rest. At the end of that year in Fairhope, Elizabeth graduated from high school. I have a vision of her standing in her white graduation dress in the garden where Grandma was sitting. I am sure that Grandma felt that her hardest task—protecting and educating Elizabeth—was finished. She died on the way home, while she was visiting a favorite niece in Ohio.

The closest friends I have made all through life have been people who also grew up close to a loved and loving grandmother or grandfather. 🌼

FAMILIES FROM HISTORY

Family Life in the White House

from *Upstairs at the White House* by J. B. West

We discovered soon after they moved in that the Trumans had an extraordinarily close and stable family life, one that they had obviously enjoyed for a long time, and that gave strength to them all.

When Mr. Truman ascended to the Presidency, he and his wife had already settled into a simple pattern of living that reflected their small-town background, their age, and their economic status. Even in his three months as Vice President, Mr. Truman had been able to live quietly out of the spotlight, as he had when he was the U.S. Senator from Missouri. I think this was partly because Franklin Roosevelt was such an overpowering figure, partly because World War II, not personality, was the all-consuming public interest, but mostly because the Trumans preferred it that way.

The Trumans were the closest family who lived in the White House during the twenty-eight years I worked there. Some of the staff called them the "Three Musketeers," as they obviously enjoyed each other's company very much. They were essentially very private people who didn't show affection in public. But they did everything together—read, listened to the radio, played the piano, and mostly talked to each other. They had few private dinner parties; they ate informally together, in the third-floor solarium or, in good weather, on the South Portico. They lived as simply at 1600 Pennsylvania Avenue as they had at 4700 Connecticut Avenue in Independence, Missouri. . . .

Perhaps they were following a lifetime habit of private pleasures, perhaps they were limited in their activities by their personal finances, perhaps they felt bound by wartime austerity, or perhaps, as I said, they just preferred it that way. I rather think the President took very seriously the burden of office that had fallen on his shoulders, and, not being a young man, directed his private life first and foremost to the preservation of his health.

He was deeply aware of the role then being assumed by the United States in reshaping the world, and of his own predominant responsibility in these broadened international responsibilities. At home, the entire economy had to be restructured, as he had to formulate policies for converting from war to peace. He had no Vice President. He had to stay alive and keenly alert, if he were to cope with his job.

"A man in my position has a public duty to keep himself in good condition," he said. "You can't be mentally fit unless you're physically fit."

Our lives changed drastically to fit his Spartan regimen. He was up every morning at 5:30. I reported in at 6, and often met him heading for his brisk morning walk.

"It's the best part of the day," he told me often, as he took off, 120 paces a minute, marching his Secret Service agents around Washington for an hour, in heat, rain, or freezing cold. His walks were well publicized, but they were only the warmup of President Truman's daily physical fitness program. He went from his walk to the swimming pool, where he worked out with Master Sergeant Gaspar, the physical therapist.

From the pool—where he swam with his glasses on—to the rowing machines, to the exercise machines, and twenty-five sit-ups. Then to the sweatbox, and back to the pool. Pretty soon he had certain overweight mem-

bers of his staff going through the same routine.

Punctuality was the order for the Trumans. A hearty family breakfast was served at eight, and he expected Mrs. Truman and Margaret to be up and at the table with him. After breakfast, they all went to work.

I saw Mrs. Truman at nine every morning in her little office. She sat behind her desk, dressed for the day, decorous to a degree, often wearing a simply tailored house-dress. . . .

Mrs. Truman explained their diets from the beginning. There was to be no salt used, because she suffered from high blood pressure. We even had to remove the water softening system from the cold-water plumbing, because it contained sodium.

The President was on a high-protein, low-calorie diet, and they shunned rich sauces and desserts. It was mostly plain, meat-and-vegetables, American food. . . . .

After the menus, we got down to business, as Mrs. Truman was very conscious of economy in housekeeping. She kept her own books, went over bills with a finetooth comb, and wrote every check herself.

It was during these morning sessions that I began to appreciate Mrs. Truman's humor. Her wit was dry, laconic, incisive and very funny. It's difficult to capture in words because it was so often silent. . . .

Although the Trumans sought informality, the traditions of waiting on Presidents are strong ones, so two butlers, dressed formally in black, served three very informal Trumans.

In good weather, dinner was out on the South Portico, overlooking the Washington Monument, again served formally, although

the President fed the squirrel between courses.

After dinner, the Trumans often watched movies, mainly because Margaret, a movie buff, often implored her parents to join her. Her mother spent more time with her in the theater than her father did, although I dare say neither of them sat through "The Scarlet Pimpernel" sixteen times, as Margaret did.

Mrs. Truman and her daughter played ping-pong in the third-floor hall; they played bridge on the second floor with some of Margaret's friends; they bowled in the new bowling alley.

But mainly, as a family, they talked to each other. 🖾

Family Vacations

WORLD FAMOUS TREE HOUSE, LILLEY REDWOOD PARK, REDWOOD HIGHWAY, CALIFORNIA

Souvenir postcards made their first appearance at the 1893 World's Columbian Exposition. They immediately became popular with vacationers everywhere, who wanted to take back a visual record of their travels but found personal photography too complicated, too difficult, or too expensive.

In 1917, more than fifty thousand visitors toured America's National Parks by automobile. Ten years later, the number of visitors had soared to four hundred thousand.

LITTLE CHIEF MOUNTAIN, ST. MARY LAKE

1940, the average cost of an automobile was $1,200. Gas cost 14 to 19 cents per gallon.

Legendary Route 66 opened in 1932, connecting Chicago to Los Angeles by way of a 2,448 mile route that traversed the heart of middle America. The road, immortalized in songs and movies, has been mostly replaced by major interstate highways, but holds a permanent spot in the memories of Americans who crossed the country for the first time following its signs.

The Model T, called the "Universal Car," was released by Henry Ford in 1908. A replacement muffler cost a quarter, and a new fender ran the owner as much as $2.50.

Cover of Motor Magazine, May 1919

Burma Shave Signs made their debut in Minnesota, entertaining travelers with their rhyming road signs:
"Does your husband misbehave
Grunt and grumble
Rant and rave?
Shoot the brute some
Burma Shave"

The first service station road maps, given away in Pittsburgh in 1913, featured unnamed and unnumbered roads. Before road maps, there were photo-auto guides, which featured photographs of landmarks along the route. The photo guides did not last, however, as they were bulky and impossible to keep up to date.

"We are the first nation in the history of the world to go to the poor house in an automobile." Will Rogers

CRAFTS FOR THE WHOLE FAMILY

Florence loved her bonnets!

Many a quilt was made on this porch.

The house that Father built

Greta with the
dress Grandma made

Nice hat!
Jack age 2

Francine and the
bow she made

Picnic Blanket

Designed by Nancy J. Worrell

At first glance, this picnic cloth made from blue-and-white striped ticking and red-checked trim appears to be nothing more than an attractive blanket perfect to use for summer outings. Upon closer examination, however, you'll find it actually doubles as the picnic basket itself! The blanket sports four side pockets stuffed with matching red-checked napkins, and it also has room for forks, knives, and spoons.

To make a 60-inch square picnic blanket, you will need 2 yards of 60-inch blue-and-white-striped ticking, 2 yards of 45-inch red-checked cotton, and threads to match the fabric colors. Before beginning, wash, dry, and press all fabric. All seams will be half-inch.

Begin by cutting one 60-inch square from the blue and white ticking. From remaining ticking, cut four 11-inch squares for the pockets. Cut the red-checked cotton into four 18-inch squares for the napkins; with the remaining cotton, cut 1½-inch-wide bias strips, piecing as needed to a total of nine yards in length.

To make pockets, fold one 11-inch square diagonally with wrong sides facing and raw edges aligned. (The pockets will be double thickness.) Press. Next, with right sides facing and raw edges aligned, stitch bias strip to diagonal edge of pocket. Press bias strip toward outside edge and fold pocket back. Turn raw edges under one quarter inch and topstitch in place. Repeat for three remaining pockets.

To attach pockets to blanket, pin pockets to each corner of 60-inch blue and white ticking piece with right sides facing and raw edges aligned. Stitch in place along the edge of blanket. To make napkin slot, measure and mark five inches from each side of top edge of pocket. Topstitch a line at 90 degree angle from pocket top to blanket edge. (See diagram.) Repeat for three remaining pockets.

Once all pockets are attached, stitch bias strip along the edges of the blanket with right sides facing and raw edges aligned. Fold bias strip to back of blanket, turn raw edges under one quarter-inch, and topstitch in place. Finish napkin squares by turning raw edges under one quarter-inch and topstitching. Place one napkin in the center slot of each pocket.

TABLE CLOTH

POCKET

TOPSTITCHING

8"

8"

DIAGRAM FOR POCKET

CRAFTS FOR THE WHOLE FAMILY

Rosebud Picture Frame & Decorated Memento Box

Designed by Heidi T. King

A picture frame covered with delicate dried rosebuds is an elegant and creative way to display a photograph of your loved ones. Display it next to other framed photographs, sentimental bric-a-brac, or a memento box, made from an ordinary cigar box transformed into a treasure chest with decorative paper, lacy ribbon, and a few rosebuds. Tuck tiny keepsakes such as maps from family travels, tickets stubs from special events, or favorite family snapshots inside the box, preserving them to be enjoyed and remembered for years to come.

For the picture frame you'll need a hot-glue gun, clear glue sticks, newspaper, a picture frame with at least a quarter-inch border, and dried rosebuds. (Small rosebuds work best. They can be purchased already dried, or dried at home from fresh flowers.) Begin by spreading the newspaper on a flat surface. Lay the picture frame face up in the middle of the paper-covered area. Using the photograph at right as a guide, glue the rosebuds in an attractive arrangement around the border of the picture frame, beginning at the inside edge and working outward. When the front surface is covered, stand the frame and continue to glue rosebuds to sides of frame. (Set aside a few rosebuds to decorate the memento box.) Cover all but the bottom side, which must be left clear to stand the frame. When glue is dry, place photograph in frame and display.

The memento box begins with a cigar box. Gather together decorative paper to match the rosebuds on the picture frame, clear-drying craft glue, 2 yards of 1½-inch wide ribbon in a coordinating color, hot glue gun and glue sticks, and remaining rosebuds from picture frame.

Measure and cut the decorative paper to cover the cigar box, inside and out. Glue paper to box with clear drying glue and let dry completely. Next, cut a piece of ribbon to run lengthwise across box top, leaving enough extra to tuck securely under edge of box top. Hot glue the ribbon in place according to the photograph.

To make the bow, cut a piece of ribbon twice the width of the lid. Hot glue the ends together to form a loop. Center the glued ends of ribbon and press them to opposite side of loop, forming 2 equal-sized, smaller loops. Repeat this process

116

with a piece of ribbon 4 inches shorter than the original. Center the smaller loops on top of the larger and hot glue a scrap of ribbon around the center. Hot glue this one large, 4-looped bow to the strip of ribbon on the box top. Top the bow with remaining rosebuds.

Patriotic Pocket Quilt

Designed by Nancy J. Worrell

The centuries-old art of quilting was revitalized by thrifty early American women who saved each scrap of fabric, regardless of its color or shape or material. Later, they stitched these pieces into a colorful, cozy coverlet for a child's bed or for added warmth on their own bed on a cold winter's night. Today, quilting remains popular, although more as a leisure-time hobby than as a necessary chore. And modern techniques have made the job of completing a beautiful quilt the pleasant task of several hours rather than the work of several weeks or months.

This Patriotic Pocket Quilt can be stitched together in a minimum amount of time. What's more, this contemporary version of the timeless patchwork quilt has a clever pocket added, making it convenient to carry along on all types of family outings, from picnics, to ball games, to summer vacations.

To make the 51-inch quilt pictured here you will need 1½ yards each of 60-inch red cotton print and 60-inch blue cotton print, thread to match each of the fabric colors, 2 pieces of thin quilt batting (one 51-inch square and one 21-inch square), a #18 tapestry needle, one skein of 4-ply red acrylic yarn, and 9 yards of red double-fold bias tape.

Before beginning work on the quilt, wash, dry, and press all fabric. Begin by cutting fabric squares. From the red cotton print cut one 44-inch square, four 45-x-5-inch strips, and four 5-inch squares. In addition, cut one 17-inch square and one 5-x-20-inch strip. From the blue print, cut one 44-inch square, four 45-x-5-inch strips, and four 5-inch squares. From the remaining blue print, cut one 16-x-20-inch piece, two 3-x-20-inch strips, and two 3-x-17-inch strips.

To make side borders of quilt, with right sides facing and raw edges aligned, stitch one 44-x-5-inch red strip to one side of the 44-inch blue square; then stitch another 44-x-5-inch red strip to the opposite side of the blue square.

For the top and bottom borders of quilt, with right sides facing and raw edges aligned, stitch a 5-inch blue square to each end of a 44-x-5-inch red strip; repeat to make a matching red and blue strip. With right sides facing and raw edges aligned, stitch a red and blue strip to the top and bottom edges of the 44-inch blue square. Press seams toward borders.

Make backing borders in same manner as above, reversing colors and attaching to the red 44-inch square.

To assemble quilt, stack the red backing (right side down), the 51-inch bat-

ting, and the blue top (right side up). Baste around edges.

Measure and mark tacking points on quilt top at evenly spaced intervals. Using the #18 tapestry needle and the red yarn, tack the quilt layers together at each marked tacking point, leaving 1½ inches on each end of yarn. Tie the yarn ends together securely.

To make pocket top, with right sides facing and raw edges aligned, stitch a 17-inch strip of blue print to each side edge of a 17-inch square of red print. Next, stitch a 20-inch strip of blue print to top and bottom edges in the same manner. Press all seams toward borders. To make pocket backing, with right sides facing and raw edges aligned, stitch the remaining red strip to a 20-inch

CRAFTS FOR THE WHOLE FAMILY

side of the blue pocket.

Stack the backing (right side down), batting, and top (right side up). Baste around edges.

Trim excess batting from the edge of the quilt pocket. Bind the edges of the quilt pocket with double-fold bias tape.

To complete the quilt, center the pocket at the bottom of quilt, 16 inches from each side edge, matching border of pocket backing with border of quilt top. Whipstitch the pocket to top along 3 edges, leaving the outside edge open.

To store and carry the quilt, fold it into thirds, turn the pocket backing to the outside, and stuff the quilt into the pocket.

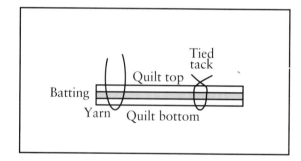

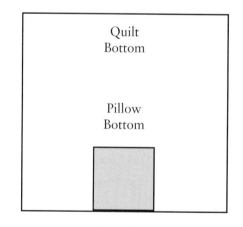

Aprons for Grandma and Her Little Helper

Designed by Nancy J. Worrell

A few snips with the scissors and a bit of sewing turns ordinary kitchen towels into charming aprons for grandmother and her little helper. Inexpensive and quite easy to put together, these aprons are the perfect project to get your own "little helper" interested in both sewing and cooking.

With the help of your child, grandchild, or other small friend, choose 3 brightly colored 27-x-19-inch plaid cotton dish towels. Also purchase 6 yards of double-fold bias tape and thread in matching colors. The directions are written to make both aprons at the same time; the child may follow along, working on his or her own project.

For the adult's apron, fold one towel in half lengthwise and, following the Diagram for Adult, cut a curved edge for the armhole. Repeat with a second towel for the child's apron, following Diagram for Child. Zigzag stitch the edges of both towels after cutting to prevent raveling. For the adult's pocket, cut a 7½-x-19-inch strip from the bottom of the third towel. For child's pocket, cut a 6½-inch strip lengthwise from across the bottom of the child's towel. To attach the pocket to adult's apron, with raw edges aligned, lay right side of pocket on wrong side of apron bottom and stitch together along bottom edge. (Unstitched edge of pocket is finished edge of towel.) Press seam open. Turn pocket to apron front and stitch together along sides. Mark the pocket into thirds and topstitch pocket to apron vertically in 2 places to make 3 pockets. Repeat for child's apron.

To finish the adult's apron, topstitch the long edges of 24 inches of bias tape together for a tie. Do not cut. With sewing machine needle still in place, begin at one end of one armhole and bind edge with double-fold bias tape. Continue topstitching bias tape to the other end of armhole. Do not bind top edge of the apron, but continue to stitch 24 inches of bias tape along long edges for neck loop. Do not cut. With sewing machine needle still in place, bind edge of remaining armhole with double-fold bias tape. Finish by topstitching 24 inches of bias tape along long edges for a tie. Finish the child's apron in the same manner, leaving 22-inch tails for ties and an 18-inch neck loop.

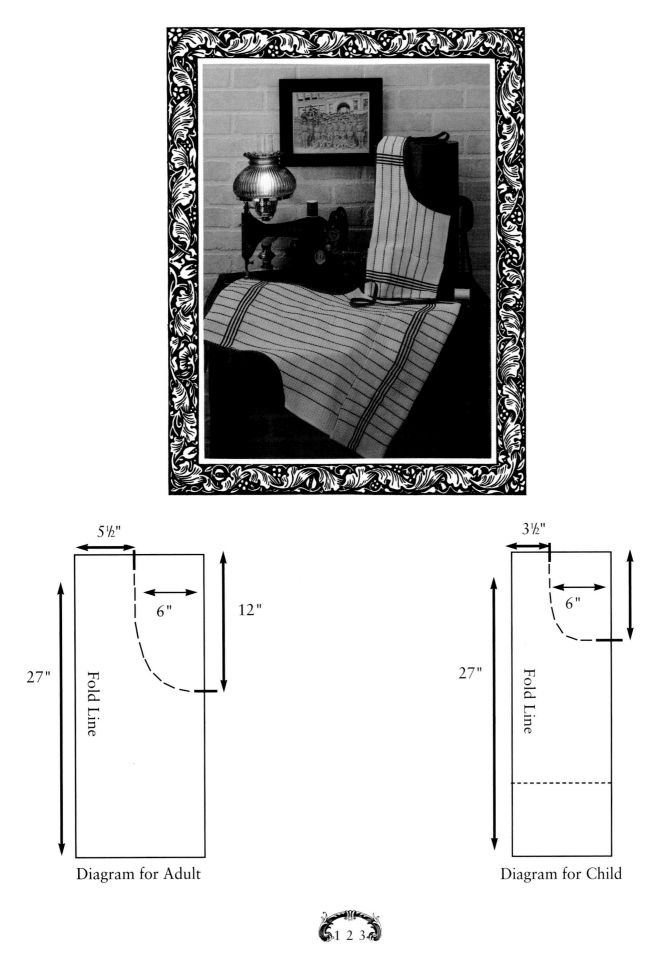

5½"

6"

12"

27"

Fold Line

Diagram for Adult

3½"

6"

27"

Fold Line

Diagram for Child

Old-Fashioned Wool Penny Rug

Designed by Nancy J. Worrell

Penny Rugs, so named because of the round copper coins used as templates, became fashionable in the middle of the nineteenth century as a colorful and practical use for fabric scraps from other projects. Made from scraps of wool too small to braid into a rug, the colorful remnants were cut into geometric shapes, layered on a larger piece of fabric, and then stitched together with a decorative buttonhole stitch.

The penny rug featured here employs the same time-tested techniques on a slightly larger scale to create a colorful wall hanging or attractive table runner.

To make the rug pictured here, you will need a 26½-by-12¼-inch piece of black wool, black sewing thread, a quarter-yard each of royal blue, magenta, black, and forest green wool, liquid ravel preventer, clear-drying craft glue, 3 skeins of #942 DMC embroidery floss, and a #18 tapestry needle.

To begin the rug, turn the edges of the large black wool piece under ½ inch two times and whipstitch in place using black thread. Press the seams.

From the royal blue wool, cut twenty-two 2½-inch circles and eight 1¼-inch circles. From the magenta wool, cut 18 of the larger-sized circles and 12 of the smaller. From black wool, cut 25 of the smaller-sized circles. From the forest green wool, cut 15 large circles and 10 small.

Apply the liquid ravel preventer around the edge of each circle and allow to dry.

Referring to the photograph on the next page, glue the smaller circles to the centers of the larger, matching colors exactly as indicated on the chart. Allow to dry.

Using three strands of embroidery floss and the #18 tapestry needle, buttonhole stitch around the edge of each of the small wool circles.

Again referring to the photograph for color placement, position the glued circle pairs on the black wool base. Position the large circles so that they touch each other on four sides. The outside circles should overlap the edges of the base one-quarter inch. Once placement is correct, glue all circles in place. Allow to dry thoroughly.

To finish the rug, buttonhole stitch around the edge of each large circle using three strands of embroidery floss and the tapestry needle. After stitching is complete, press rug flat.

Lacy Pew Baby

Designed by Martha K. Bonner

Desperate to keep squirming children quiet during church services, mothers of the nineteenth century created "pew babies" by tying their handkerchiefs into small, lacy dolls. Although the original handkerchief babies consisted only of knots tied for arms and a head, later models were embellished with lace edging around the fabric and embroidered with facial details and decorations at the hem. This sweet doll is a rendition of the traditional babies, with embroidered details and seed pearls scattered randomly along the bottom of the dress.

To make your own beautiful lacy pew baby, you will need one 15-inch square white cotton handkerchief, one 10-inch square white cotton handkerchief, 2 yards of 2-inch wide pregathered lace trim, 2 yards $^1/_8$-inch wide green satin ribbon, threads to match the fabrics, black embroidery floss, a tapestry needle, small seed beads in red, green, and gold, and a small amount of stuffing.

To begin, finish the handkerchiefs by machine stitching lace trim around the edges of each using white sewing thread. On the 10-inch handkerchief, machine stitch green ribbon around edge at the top of the lace.

For the eyes, refer to the first diagram and stemstitch with black embroidery floss. For skirt decoration, stitch seed beads around edge of 15-inch handkerchief using photograph as a guide. Make the head by placing a small amount of stuffing under wrong side of 15-inch handkerchief, centering eyes at top front of head. Secure head by tying a 12-inch piece of green ribbon around handkerchief below stuffing.

For arms, tie a 12-inch piece of ribbon in a bow, 2 inches from each side corner of handkerchief. For shawl, refer to the second diagram and fold right side of one end of 10-inch handkerchief 3½ inches, then fold wrong side of folded end back to edge of handkerchief 1¾ inches. With lace positioned directly above eyes, place shawl on doll and handstitch around head into place.

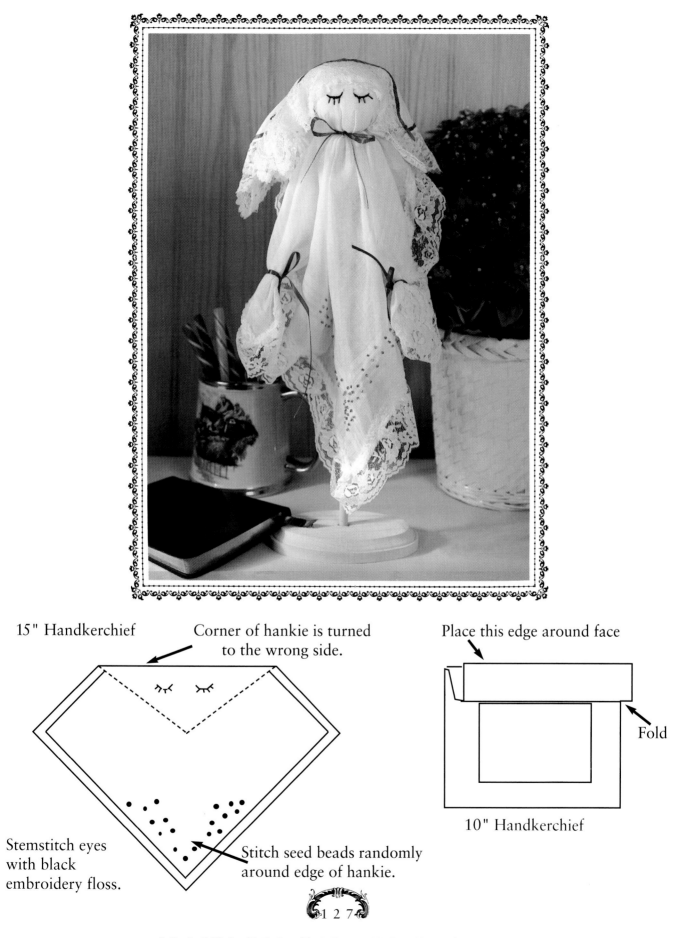

15" Handkerchief

Corner of hankie is turned
to the wrong side.

Place this edge around face

Fold

10" Handkerchief

Stemstitch eyes
with black
embroidery floss.

Stitch seed beads randomly
around edge of hankie.

A Cross-Stitch Sampler

Designed and stitched by Teri Zweifel

Samplers have been a part of American family life throughout our history. With help from Mother, young girls put together their first sampler as proof of their mastery of decorative stitching. Originally, samplers featured the alphabet and showed off a wide array of complex stitches. This modern version is much less complex, only requiring mastery of the simple counted cross-stitch, yet it captures the charm and the beauty of the old-fashioned American sampler.

Finished design size: $6^9/_{16}$-x $10^1/_4$- inches. (Length=169 stitches; width=109 stitches)
Finished project size: 9 x $12^3/_4$ inches
Materials: 13-x-9-inch, 28 count, champagne-colored linen   (*Note:* Measurements include 3-inch framing allowance on all sides.); DMC thread (see color chart); embroidery needle; scissors; embroidery hoop. (*Fabric options:* aida 11ct, $15^4/_{11}$-x-$9^{10}/_{11}$; aida 14ct, $12^1/_{14}$-x-$8^5/_{14}$; aida 18ct, $9^7/_8$-x-$18^1/_{18}$, aida 22ct, $7^{15}/_{22}$-x-$4^{21}/_{22}$.)

Preparing fabric: Prevent raveling by binding edges with masking tape or by machine stitching $^1/_8$ inch from all edges.

Finding pattern and fabric centers: The horizontal and vertical centers of the pattern are indicated by arrows. The cross (+) indicates design center. To locate fabric center, fold fabric in half, forming a rectangle. Mark crease with pins or with a tailor's pen. Now fold rectangular shape into a square: mark crease as before. Open fabric flat and baste between pins/pen marks, dividing fabric into quarters. Fabric center is located where basting stitches intersect.

Cross-stitching: (*Note:* Use 2 strands of thread and work all stitches over 2 horizontal and vertical fabric threads.) Matching design and fabric centers, begin stitching on the letter closest to the center of the pattern. Begin counting blocks from design and fabric centers; count off the corresponding number of blocks to be left blank until design begins. Make the first "X" by pulling thread through from wrong side in lower left corner of block. Leave three quarters of an inch of thread dangling on underside. Carry needle diagonally across two fabric threads to opposite corner, inserting it through from front to back.

To complete cross make another stitch from the opposite corner, covering the first stitch and securing the dangling thread from behind. Continue as instructed, keeping all stitches uniform in size and shape. After making a few stitches, place fabric in embroidery hoop, keeping work area centered and pulled tight. Finish the entire project in like fashion, changing thread colors as the pattern indicates.

ABCDEFGHIJK
LMNOPQRSTU
VWXYZ

abcdefghijklmn

opqrstuvw

xyz

Home is where
the heart is!

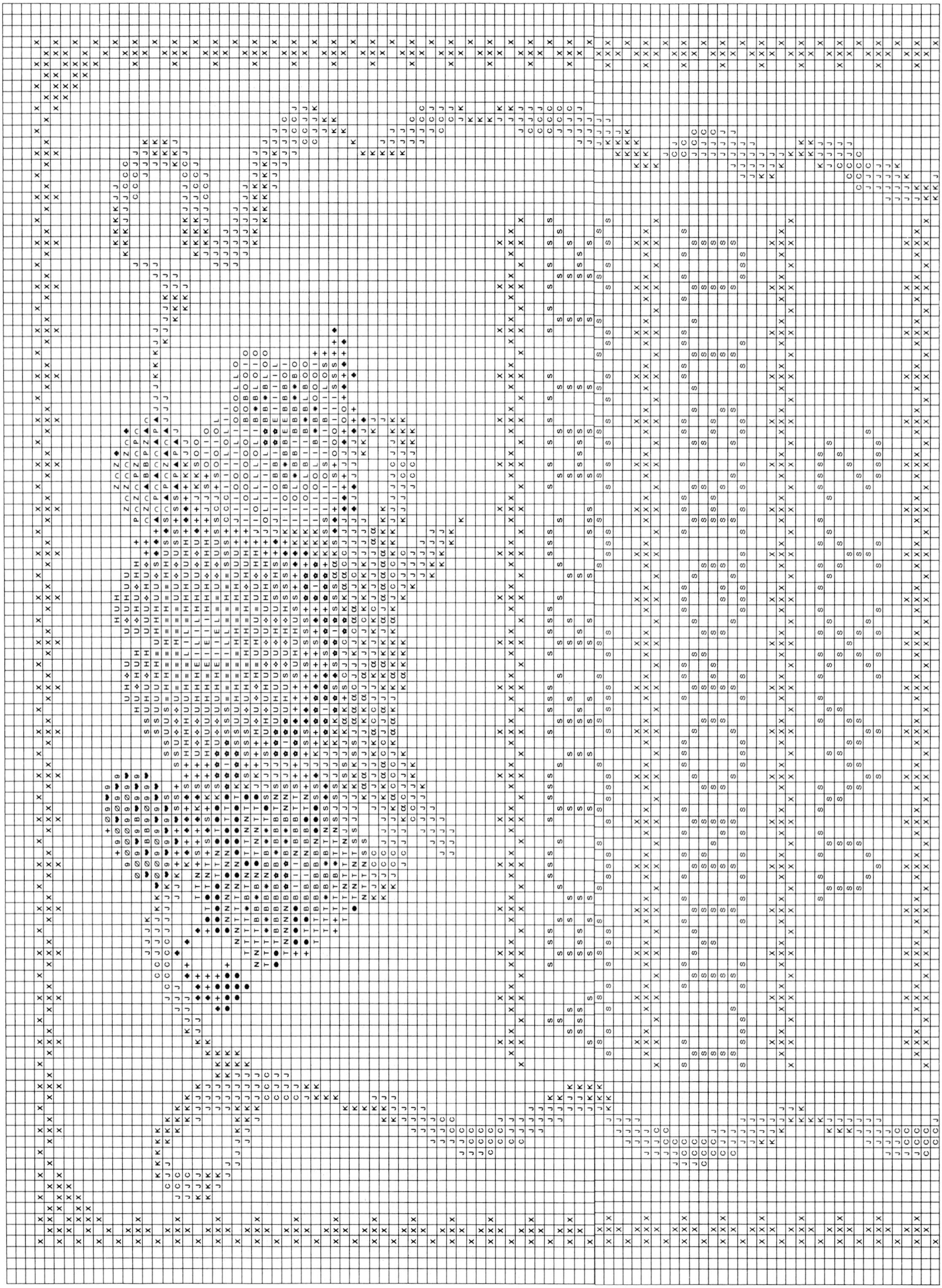

X	ECRU
▲	DMC 208
∩	DMC 209
Z	DMC 211
B	DMC 310
P	DMC 340
✳	DMC 535
α	DMC 600
K	DMC 602
J	DMC 603
C	DMC 604
✛	DMC 702
♣	DMC 703
♥	DMC 718
I	DMC 727
O	DMC 729
E	DMC 743
L	DMC 782
●	DMC 796
T	DMC 798
N	DMC 813
S	DMC 986
9	DMC 3608
∅	DMC 3609
≡	DMC 3685
H	DMC 3687
U	DMC 3688
✧	DMC 3689

The Home

The Sears, Roebuck & Company catalogue first appeared in 1887. The "wish book," as it was soon known, was an indispensible item in the American home, selling everything from children's clothing to musical instruments to house building kits.

In 1900, there were 16,188,000 families in America; the average family size was 4.7 persons. Sixty percent of those families lived on farms or in small rural towns.

American families spent a great deal of time together in the 30s, and most of that was devoted to radio listening. In 1937 the average American family spent four and a half hours a day listening to the radio.

THE CRESCENT
Described on
Page 26

Honor Bilt

MODERN HOM

Sears, Roebuck and
CHICAGO · PHILADELPHIA

By 1924, ninety percent of American families owned an electric iron.

SEVEN ROOMS AND BIG PORCH

Honor Bilt
The Albion
No. P.3227 "Already Cut" and Fitted
$2,515.00

Can be built on a lot 32 feet wide

SECOND FLOOR PLAN

Page 81

The Greatest Building Proposition!

If Your Monthly Rent Is	You Have Spent Counting Interest at 6%		
	In 7 Years	In 10 Years	In 15 Years
$25.00	$2,518.13	$ 3,954.20	$ 6,982.23
35.00	3,525.38	5,535.88	9,775.82
40.00	4,029.00	6,326.32	11,172.88
50.00	5,036.25	7,908.40	13,965.46
60.00	6,043.50	9,490.08	16,768.54
70.00	7,050.75	11,071.76	19,551.64
80.00	8,058.00	12,652.46	22,345.76
90.00	9,065.25	14,234.72	25,138.34

Families first woke up to the luxury of an electric pop-up toaster in 1926

In 1931, most families still had a mother who stayed at home, thanks in part to a ban on working wives in seventy-five percent of American cities.

In 1920, an electric vacuum cleaner could be had for forty dollars. Most vacuums were bought on installment, with a downpayment of two dollars and then four dollars a month until payment was complete.

"THE OLD" AND "THE NEW"

THE WOMAN'S FRIEND

Look here, Weary Woman, there is Rest for You!
STEAM WILL DO YOUR WASHING!

THE
STEAM WASHER
OR
WOMAN'S FRIEND.
PRICE, - $10.00.

The Latest, the Cheapest, the Best—No Rubbing, no Pounding, no Turning or Tearing, no clumsy Cylinder, and no $20 or $30 expense. Steam does it all! Nothing like it in use. Call and see it in operation.

AT   Or Address J. C. Tilton, Patentee, Pittsburgh, Pa.

A FEW SPECIAL AGENTS WANTED!
A GOOD OPENING FOR MEN OUT OF EMPLOYMENT WHO REALLY WANT TO MAKE MONEY.
SPECIAL AND GENERAL AGENT.

JOHN JACOBIN AND HIS WIFE JANE ON WASH DAY.

ar-time rationing allowed each mily twenty-eight ounces of eat, four ounces of butter, four ounds of cheese, and no sliced ead each week.

he woman who doesn't want to ake a home is undermining a tion."   Mrs. Thomas Edison

A 1908 survey found that cleaning the average American family home required twenty-seven hours of work.

A FAMILY SINGALONG

Thelma loves piano & sings as well. Anne is six here.

Grandpa plays the banjo. Jimmy just plays.

Auntie Pearl with Gracie.
Auntie sings Soprano.

Sarah has a beautiful
voice. Here she is with
Jeannie + Tommy.

Uncle Ray (driving) sang
Barbershop.

The day we gained a Bass.
Mary with new husband, Robert,
Helen + Tom.

I Want a Girl

William Dillon

Harry Von Tilzer

1. When I was a boy my moth-er oft-en said to me: "Get mar-ried, boy, and
2. By the old mill stream there sits a coup-le old and gray, Though years have rolled a-

see how hap-py you will be," I have looked all o-ver, but no
way their hearts are young to - day, Moth - er dear looks up at Dad with

girl - ie can I find Who seems to be just like the lit - tle girl I have in
love light in her eye, He steals a kiss, a fond em - brace while ev - 'ning breez-es

mind, I will have to look a - round un - til the right one I have found.
sigh, There're as hap-py as can be, so that's the kind of love for me.

I want a girl, just like the girl that mar - ried

AMERICAN FAMILY TREASURY

A FAMILY SINGALONG

Sweet Rosie O'Grady

Maude Nugent

Sweet Ro - sie O' - Gra - dy, My dear lit - tle

Rose,_____ She's my stea - dy la - dy,

Most ev - 'ry - one knows,_____ And when we are mar -

ried, How hap - py we'll be;_____ I love sweet Ro - sie O' -

Gra - dy, And Ro - sie O' - Gra - dy loves me._____

Oh You Beautiful Doll

A. Seymour Brown

Nat. D. Ayer

Oh! you beau-ti-ful doll,___ you great, big beau-ti-ful doll!___

Let___ me put my arms a-bout you, I___ could nev-er live with-out you;

Oh! you beau-ti-ful doll,___ You great, big beau-ti-ful doll!___ If you

ev-er leave___ me how my heart will ache,___ I want to hug___ you but I fear you'd break.___

Oh, oh, oh, oh, Oh, you beau-ti-ful doll!

A FAMILY SINGALONG

Mary's a Grand Old Name

George M. Cohan

For it is Ma - ry, Ma - ry, plain as an - y name can

be; But with pro - pri - e - ty, so - ci - e - ty will say Ma -

rie. But it was Ma - ry, Ma - ry,

long be - fore the fash - ions came, And there is some - thing there that

sounds so square, It's a grand old name.

AMERICAN FAMILY TREASURY

When You and I Were Young, Maggie

V.A. Butterfield

1. I wan-dered to-day to the hill, Mag-gie, To watch the scene be-
2. They say I am fee-ble with age, Mag-gie, My steps less spright-ly than

low; The creek and the creak-ing old mill, Mag-gie, As
then; My face is a well-writ-ten page, Mag-gie, But

we used to 'long, long a-go. The green grove is gone from the
time a-lone was the pen. They say we are a-ged and

hill, Mag-gie, Where first the dais-ies sprung, The
gray, Mag-gie, Where Spray first by the white break-ers flung, But to

creak-ing old mill is still, Mag-gie, Since you and I were young.
me you're as fair as you were, Mag-gie, When you and I were young.

A FAMILY SINGALONG

Let Me Call You Sweetheart

Beth Slater Whitson

Leo Friedman

1. I am dream-ing Dear of you, Day by
2. Long-ing for you all the while More and

day_____ Dream-ing when the skies are blue,
more_____ Long-ing when for the sun-ny smile

When they're gray;_____ When the sil-v'ry moon-light
I a dore; Birds are sing-ing far and

gleams Still I wan-der on in dreams In a land of
near Ros-es bloom-ing ev-'ry-where You, a-lone, my

love, it seems cheer, Just You with you._____
heart it can Just You just you._____

Let me call you, "Sweet - heart" I'm in love with you

Let me hear you whis - per that you love me

too Keep the love - light glow - ing in your

eyes so true Let me call you

"Sweet - heart" I'm in love with you.

A FAMILY SINGALONG

Come, Josephine in My Flying Machine

Alfred Bryan

Fred. Fischer

1. Oh,   say!   let us fly, dear. Where,   kid?
2. One,   two,   now we're off, dear. Say   you,

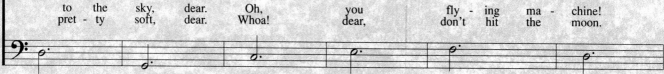

to the sky, dear. Oh,   you   fly - ing ma - chine!
pret - ty soft, dear. Whoa!   dear,   don't hit the moon.

Jump   in   Miss Jo - seph - ine. Ship A - hoy!   Oh,
No,   dear,   not yet but soon. You for me,   Oh,

joy! what a feel - ing. Where,   boy?   In the ceil - ing. Ho,
gee! you're a fly kid. Not   me,   I'm a sky kid. Gee!

high,   hoop - la! we fly to the sky   so   high._____
I'm   up in the air a - bout you   for   fair._____

AMERICAN FAMILY TREASURY

Come, Jo - seph - ine, in my fly-ing ma - chine, Go - ing up, she goes! up she

goes! Bal - ance your - self like a bird on a beam, In the air she goes;

there she goes! Up, up, a lit - tle bit high - er.

Oh, my! the moon is on fire._____ Come, Jo - seph - ine in my

fly - ing ma - chine, Go - ing up, all on, "Good - bye!"_____

1 4 5

A FAMILY SINGALONG

When You Were Sweet Sixteen

James Thornton

AMERICAN FAMILY TREASURY

CHORUS

hold you in my arms just once a - gain. I
love you as the sun - shine once loves the morn.

love you as I nev - er lov'd be - fore, Since

first I met you on the vil - lage green. Come

to me or my dream of love is o'er. I

love you as I lov'd you, When you were sweet, when you were sweet six-teen.

A FAMILY SINGALONG

Down by the Old Mill Stream

Tell Taylor

1. My darl - ing, I am dream - ing, of the days gone
2. The old mill wheel is si - lent, and has fall - en

by, When you and I were sweet - hearts, be - neath the sum - mer
down, The old oak tree has with - ered and lies there on the

sky; Your hair has turned to sil - ver, the
ground; While you and I are sweet - hearts, the

gold has fad - ed too; But still I will re -
same as days of yore; Al - though we've been to -

mem - ber where I first met you. Down by the
geth - er for - ty years and more.

AMERICAN FAMILY TREASURY

old   mill   stream,_____ where I first   met   you,_____

___ With your eyes   of   blue,_____ dressed in ging - ham

too,_____ It was there   I   knew_____ that you

loved   me   true._____ You were six - teen,_____ my vil - lage

queen,_____ by the old   mill   stream._____

A FAMILY SINGALONG

Put on Your Old Grey Bonnet

Stanley Murphy

Percy Wenrich

1. On the old farm house ve - ran - da There sat Si - las and Mi - ran - da, Think-ing of the
2. It was in the same old bon - net with the same blue rib - bon on it, In the old shay,

days gone by.___ Said he, "Dear - ie, don't be wea - ry, you were al - ways bright and
by his side,___ That he drove her up to Dov - er thro' the same old fields of

cheer - y, But a tear, dear, dims your eye."___ Said
clov - er, To be - come his hap - py bride.___ The

she, "they're tears of glad - ness, Si - las, they're not tears of sad - ness. It is fif - ty years to-
birds were sweet - ly sing - ing And the same old bells were ring - ing, As they passed the quaint old

day since we were wed."___ Then the old man's dim eyes bright-ened and his
church where they were wed.___ And that night when stars were gleam - ing, The old

stern old heart it light-en'd as he turn'd to her and said,_____ "Put on your
cou-ple lay a dream-ing Dream-ing the words he said,_____

old grey bon-net with the blue rib-bon on it while I

hitch old Dob-bin to the shay;_____ And through the

fields of clo-ver we'll drive up to Dov-er on our

gold - en Wed - ding day!"_____

A FAMILY SINGALONG

My Wild Irish Rose

Chauncey Olcott

1. If you lis - ten I'll sing you a sweet lit - tle song, Of a flow - er that's
2. They may sing of their ro - ses, which by oth - er names, Would— smell just as

now dropt— and dead;— Yet dear - er to me, yes, than all of its
sweet - ly,— they say.— But I know that my Rose,— would nev - er con -

mates, Tho'— each holds a - loft its— proud head.— 'Twas giv - en to me by a
sent, To have that sweet name tak - en— a - way.— Her glan - ces are shy when—

girl that I know, Since we've met, faith I've known no re - pose,— She is dear - er by
e'er I pass by, The— bow - er, where my true love grows,— And my one wish has

far than the world's bright - est star, And I call her my wild I - rish Rose.—
been that some day I may win The— heart of my wild I - rish Rose.— My

AMERICAN FAMILY TREASURY

A FAMILY SINGALONG

By the Light of the Silvery Moon

Ed. Madden

Gus Edwards

1. Place park, scene dark, Sil - v'ry moon is shin - ing thro' the trees;
2. Act two, scene new, Ros - es bloom - ing all a - round the place;

Cast two, me, you,
Cast three, you, me,

Sound of kiss - es float - ing on the breeze. Act one,
Preach - er with a sol - emn look - ing face. Choir sings,

be - gun, Di - a - logue, "Where would you like to spoon?"
bell rings, Preach - er: "You are wed for - ev - er - more."

My cue, with you, Un - der-neath the sil - v'ry moon. By the
Act two, all through, Ev - 'ry night the same en - core.

AMERICAN FAMILY TREASURY

light _____ of the sil - ver - y moon, _____

___ I want to spoon, _____ To my hon - ey I'll

croon love's tune, Hon - ey - moon _____ keep a - shin - ing in

June, _____ Your sil - v'ry beams will bring love dreams, We'll be cud - dling

soon, _____ By the sil - ver - y moon. _____

A FAMILY SINGALONG

Fashion

"Her skirts have just reached her very trim and pretty ankles; her hair, coiled upon her skull, has just exposed the ravishing whiteness of her neck. A charming creature! There is something trim and trig and confident about her. She is easy in her manners. There is music in her laugh. She is youth, she is hope, she is romance—she is wisdom!"
    H. L. Mencken

In 1921 a law was proposed in Utah making it illegal for a woman to wear a skirt more than three inches above her ankle.

NO·VISIBLE·MEANS·OF·SUPPORT!

In the first decade of the twentieth century, American women spent fourteen million dollars per year on corsets, which were a daily dress requirement for girls over the age of fourteen.

BUTTERICK & CO'S QUARTERLY REPORT OF NEW YORK FASHIONS.
FOR SALE HERE
PRINCIPAL OFFICE, 888 BROADWAY, NEW-YORK.

"There has been a change for the worse during the past year in feminine dress, dancing, manners, and general moral standards. One should realize the serious ethical consequences of immodesty in girls' dress."
from the Pittsburgh Observer, 1922

Liberty
A Weekly for the Whole Family
5¢
WEEK ENDING JUNE 5, 1926

The Drug-Store Cow Boy

In this issue
"No Food With My Meals"
By
FANNIE HURST
Also
P. G. Wodehouse
Edwin Balmer
Finley Peter Dunne
Mary Heaton Vorse
Francis Ouimet

In 1942, the sale of trousers for women increased five to ten times over the previous year.

In 1925, the popular Charleston flare dress sold for $1.58 at Gimbels in New York.

Much of women's fashion in the early years of the century was dictated by the drawings of Charles Dana Gibson, whose beautiful Gibson girls were the role models for most young American girls.

Author Index

Title Index

2 B
3 C
4 D
5 E
6 F
7 G
8 H
9 I
0 J